Processes of Constitutional Decisionmaking

2019 Supplement

2019 Supplement

Processes of Constitutional Decisionmaking

Cases and Materials

Seventh Edition

Prepared by Jack M. Balkin

Paul Brest
Professor of Law, Emeritus and Former Dean
Stanford Law School
and President, The William and Flora Hewlett Foundation

Sanford Levinson
W. St. John Garwood & W. St. John Garwood, Jr.
Centennial Chair in Law
University of Texas Law School

Jack M. Balkin
Knight Professor of Constitutional Law
and the First Amendment
Yale Law School

Akhil Reed Amar
Sterling Professor of Law and Political Science
Yale Law School

Reva B. Siegel
Nicholas deB. Katzenbach Professor of Law
Yale Law School

Published by Wolters Kluwer in New York.

Wolters Kluwer Legal & Regulatory U.S. serves customers worldwide with CCH, Aspen Publishers, and Kluwer Law International products. (www.WKLegaledu.com)

To contact Customer Service, e-mail customer.service@wolterskluwer.com, call 1-800-234-1660, fax 1-800-901-9075, or mail correspondence to:

    Wolters Kluwer
    Attn: Order Department
    PO Box 990
    Frederick, MD 21705

Printed in the United States of America.

1 2 3 4 5 6 7 8 9 0

ISBN 978-1-5438-0934-3

About Wolters Kluwer Legal & Regulatory U.S.

Wolters Kluwer Legal & Regulatory U.S. delivers expert content and solutions in the areas of law, corporate compliance, health compliance, reimbursement, and legal education. Its practical solutions help customers successfully navigate the demands of a changing environment to drive their daily activities, enhance decision quality and inspire confident outcomes.

Serving customers worldwide, its legal and regulatory portfolio includes products under the Aspen Publishers, CCH Incorporated, Kluwer Law International, ftwilliam.com, and MediRegs names. They are regarded as exceptional and trusted resources for general legal and practice-specific knowledge, compliance and risk management, dynamic workflow solutions, and expert commentary.

Contents

Processes of Constitutional Decisionmaking

2019 Supplement

Part Two

Constitutional Adjudication in the Modern World

Insert at the end of p. 540.

In Timbs v. Indiana, 139 S.Ct. 682 (2019), the Supreme Court applied the Excessive Fines Clause of the Eighth Amendment to the States. Timbs pleaded guilty to dealing in controlled substances. The State of Indiana brought a civil forfeiture action against Timbs' vehicle, arguing that it had been used to transport heroin. The value of the vehicle was four times as great as the maximum fine assessable against him for his drug conviction.

Writing for a unanimous Supreme Court, Justice Ginsburg argued that "the protection against excessive fines has been a constant shield throughout Anglo-American history: Exorbitant tolls undermine other constitutional liberties. Excessive fines can be used, for example, to retaliate against or chill the speech of political enemies. . . . Even absent a political motive, fines may be employed 'in a measure out of accord with the penal goals of retribution and deterrence,' for 'fines are a source of revenue,' while other forms of punishment 'cost a State money.'. . . This concern is scarcely hypothetical. See Brief for American Civil Liberties Union et al. as Amici Curiae 7 ("Perhaps because they are politically easier to impose than generally applicable taxes, state and local governments nationwide increasingly depend heavily on fines and fees as a source of general revenue.")." Thus, "[t]he historical and logical case for concluding that the Fourteenth Amendment incorporates the Excessive Fines Clause is overwhelming. Protection against excessive punitive economic sanctions secured by the Clause is, to repeat, both 'fundamental to our scheme of ordered liberty' and 'deeply rooted in this Nation's history and tradition.'"

Indiana argued that although the prohibition against excessive fines was traditional, the development of civil *in rem* forfeiture laws was a comparatively recent innovation and therefore "the Clause's specific application to such forfeitures is neither fundamental nor deeply rooted." The Court rejected this argument: "In considering whether the Fourteenth Amendment incorporates a protection contained in the Bill of Rights, we ask whether the right guaranteed—not each and every particular application of that right—is fundamental or deeply rooted." The

Court had not asked, for example "whether the Free Speech Clause's application specifically to social media websites was fundamental or deeply rooted."

Justice Thomas concurred in the judgment, arguing that "the right to be free from excessive fines is one of the 'privileges or immunities of citizens of the United States' protected by the Fourteenth Amendment['s]" Privileges or Immunities Clause. Justice Gorsuch concurred, but added that "[a]s an original matter . . . the appropriate vehicle for incorporation may well be the Fourteenth Amendment's Privileges or Immunities Clause."

Chapter 6

Federalism, Separation of Powers, and National Security in the Modern Era

Insert on p. 824 immediately before Note: State Sovereign Immunity

MURPHY v. NATIONAL COLLEGIATE ATHLETIC ASSOCIATION
138 S.Ct. 1461 (2018)

[The Professional and Amateur Sports Protection Act (PASPA) makes it unlawful for a State or its subdivisions "to sponsor, operate, advertise, promote, license, or authorize by law or compact . . . a lottery, sweepstakes, or other betting, gambling, or wagering scheme based . . . on" competitive sporting events, 28 U.S.C. § 3702(1), and for "a person to sponsor, operate, advertise, or promote" those same gambling schemes if done "pursuant to the law or compact of a governmental entity," § 3702(2). But PASPA does not make sports gambling itself a federal crime. Instead, it allows the Attorney General, as well as professional and amateur sports organizations, to bring civil actions to enjoin violations.

"Grandfather" provisions allow existing forms of sports gambling to continue in four States. Another provision would have permitted New Jersey to set up a sports gambling scheme in Atlantic City within a year of PASPA's enactment. New Jersey did not take advantage of that option but later changed its mind, and passed a 2012 law legalizing sports gambling schemes in Atlantic City and at horseracing tracks. The NCAA and three major professional sports leagues successfully sued to enjoin New Jersey's new gambling law under PASPA.

In 2014 New Jersey passed a new law. Instead of affirmatively authorizing sports gambling schemes, the 2014 law simply repealed existing state-law provisions that prohibited sports gambling to the extent that they involved wagering on sporting events (1) by persons 21 years of age or older; (2) at a horseracing track or a casino or gambling house in Atlantic City; and (3) did not involve a New Jersey college team or a collegiate event taking place in the State of New Jersey. Once again, the NCAA and the sports leagues sued under PASPA. New Jersey defended on the ground that PAPSA violates the anti-commandeering principle of New York v. United States.]

Justice ALITO delivered the opinion of the Court.

II

Petitioners argue that the anti-authorization provision requires States to maintain their existing laws against sports gambling without alteration. . . . In our
view, petitioners' interpretation is correct: When a State completely or partially
repeals old laws banning sports gambling, it "authorize[s]" that activity. . . . The
concept of state "authorization" makes sense only against a backdrop of prohibition or regulation. A State is not regarded as authorizing everything that it does
not prohibit or regulate. No one would use the term in that way. For example, no
one would say that a State "authorizes" its residents to brush their teeth or eat
apples or sing in the shower. We commonly speak of state authorization only if
the activity in question would otherwise be restricted. . . .

III

A

The anticommandeering doctrine may sound arcane, but it is simply
the expression of a fundamental structural decision incorporated into the
Constitution, *i.e.,* the decision to withhold from Congress the power to issue
orders directly to the States. When the original States declared their independence, they claimed the powers inherent in sovereignty — in the words of the
Declaration of Independence, the authority "to do all . . . Acts and Things which
Independent States may of right do." The Constitution limited but did not abolish
the sovereign powers of the States, which retained "a residuary and inviolable
sovereignty.". . .

The Constitution limits state sovereignty in several ways. It directly prohibits
the States from exercising some attributes of sovereignty. See, *e.g.,* Art. I, § 10.
And the Constitution indirectly restricts the States by granting certain legislative
powers to Congress, see Art. I, § 8, while providing in the Supremacy Clause that
federal law is the "supreme Law of the Land . . . any Thing in the Constitution
or Laws of any State to the Contrary notwithstanding," Art. VI, cl. 2. This means
that when federal and state law conflict, federal law prevails and state law is
preempted.

The legislative powers granted to Congress are sizable, but they are not
unlimited. The Constitution confers on Congress not plenary legislative power
but only certain enumerated powers. Therefore, all other legislative power is
reserved for the States, as the Tenth Amendment confirms. And conspicuously
absent from the list of powers given to Congress is the power to issue direct
orders to the governments of the States. The anticommandeering doctrine simply
represents the recognition of this limit on congressional authority. . . .

New York v. United States, 505 U.S. 144 (1992) . . . concerned a federal law that
required a State, under certain circumstances, either to "take title" to low-level
radioactive waste or to "regulat[e] according to the instructions of Congress."
. . . Congress issued orders to either the legislative or executive branch of state

government (depending on the branch authorized by state law to take the actions demanded). Either way, the Court held, the provision was unconstitutional because "the Constitution does not empower Congress to subject state governments to this type of instruction." . . . "We have always understood that even where Congress has the authority under the Constitution to pass laws requiring or prohibiting certain acts, it lacks the power directly to compel the States to require or prohibit those acts." "Congress may not simply 'commandee[r] the legislative processes of the States by directly compelling them to enact and enforce a federal regulatory program.' " "Where a federal interest is sufficiently strong to cause Congress to legislate, it must do so directly; it may not conscript state governments as its agents."

Five years after *New York*, the Court applied the same principles to a federal statute requiring state and local law enforcement officers to perform background checks and related tasks in connection with applications for handgun licenses. *Printz*. Holding this provision unconstitutional, the Court put the point succinctly: "The Federal Government" may not "command the States' officers, or those of their political subdivisions, to administer or enforce a federal regulatory program." This rule applies, *Printz* held, not only to state officers with policy-making responsibility but also to those assigned more mundane tasks.

B

Our opinions in *New York* and *Printz* explained why adherence to the anticommandeering principle is important. Without attempting a complete survey, we mention several reasons that are significant here.

First, the rule serves as "one of the Constitution's structural protections of liberty." *Printz*. "The Constitution does not protect the sovereignty of States for the benefit of the States or state governments as abstract political entities." *New York*. "To the contrary, the Constitution divides authority between federal and state governments for the protection of individuals." " '[A] healthy balance of power between the States and the Federal Government [reduces] the risk of tyranny and abuse from either front.' "

Second, the anticommandeering rule promotes political accountability. When Congress itself regulates, the responsibility for the benefits and burdens of the regulation is apparent. Voters who like or dislike the effects of the regulation know who to credit or blame. By contrast, if a State imposes regulations only because it has been commanded to do so by Congress, responsibility is blurred.

Third, the anticommandeering principle prevents Congress from shifting the costs of regulation to the States. If Congress enacts a law and requires enforcement by the Executive Branch, it must appropriate the funds needed to administer the program. It is pressured to weigh the expected benefits of the program against its costs. But if Congress can compel the States to enact and enforce its program, Congress need not engage in any such analysis.

IV

The PASPA provision at issue here—prohibiting state authorization of sports gambling—violates the anticommandeering rule. That provision unequivocally dictates what a state legislature may and may not do. . . . [S]tate legislatures are put under the direct control of Congress. It is as if federal officers were installed in state legislative chambers and were armed with the authority to stop legislators from voting on any offending proposals. A more direct affront to state sovereignty is not easy to imagine.

Neither respondents nor the United States contends that Congress can compel a State to enact legislation, but they say that prohibiting a State from enacting new laws is another matter. Noting that the laws challenged in *New York* and *Printz* "told states what they must do instead of what they must not do," respondents contend that commandeering occurs "only when Congress goes beyond precluding state action and affirmatively commands it."

This distinction is empty. It was a matter of happenstance that the laws challenged in *New York* and *Printz* commanded "affirmative" action as opposed to imposing a prohibition. The basic principle—that Congress cannot issue direct orders to state legislatures—applies in either event.

Here is an illustration. PASPA includes an exemption for States that permitted sports betting at the time of enactment, but suppose Congress did not adopt such an exemption. Suppose Congress ordered States with legalized sports betting to take the affirmative step of criminalizing that activity and ordered the remaining States to retain their laws prohibiting sports betting. There is no good reason why the former would intrude more deeply on state sovereignty than the latter.

B

Respondents and the United States [rely on] *South Carolina v. Baker*, 485 U.S. 505 (1988), [in which] the [challenged] federal law . . . removed the federal tax exemption for interest earned on state and local bonds unless they were issued in registered rather than bearer form. This law did not order the States to enact or maintain any existing laws. Rather, it simply had the indirect effect of pressuring States to increase the rate paid on their bearer bonds in order to make them competitive with other bonds paying taxable interest. . . . The anticommandeering doctrine does not apply when Congress evenhandedly regulates an activity in which both States and private actors engage.

That principle formed the basis for the Court's decision in *Reno v. Condon*, 528 U.S. 141 (2000), which [upheld] a federal law restricting the disclosure and dissemination of personal information provided in applications for driver's licenses. The law applied equally to state and private actors. It did not regulate the States' sovereign authority to "regulate their own citizens."

In *Hodel*, the federal law, which involved what has been called "cooperative federalism," by no means commandeered the state legislative process. Congress enacted a statute that comprehensively regulated surface coal mining and offered States the choice of "either implement[ing]" the federal program "or else yield[ing] to a federally administered regulatory program." Thus, the federal law *allowed* but did not *require* the States to implement a federal program. "States [were] not compelled to enforce the [federal] standards, to expend any state funds, or to participate in the federal regulatory program in any manner whatsoever." If a State did not "wish" to bear the burden of regulation, the "full regulatory burden [would] be borne by the Federal Government."

Finally, in *FERC v. Mississippi*, 456 U.S. 742 (1982), the federal law in question issued no command to a state legislature. Enacted to restrain the consumption of oil and natural gas, the federal law directed state utility regulatory commissions to consider, but not necessarily to adopt, federal " 'rate design' and regulatory standards." The Court held that this modest requirement did not infringe the States' sovereign powers, but the Court warned that it had "never . . . sanctioned explicitly a federal command to the States to promulgate and enforce laws and regulations." *FERC* was decided well before our decisions in *New York* and *Printz*, and PASPA, unlike the law in *FERC*, does far more than require States to *consider* Congress's preference that the legalization of sports gambling be halted. . . .

V

[Nor does] the anti-authorization prohibition . . . constitute[] a valid preemption provision. . . . [I]n order for the PASPA provision to preempt state law, it must satisfy two requirements. First, it must represent the exercise of a power conferred on Congress by the Constitution. . . . Second, since the Constitution "confers upon Congress the power to regulate individuals, not States," *New York*, the PASPA provision at issue must be best read as one that regulates private actors.

Our cases have identified three different types of preemption—"conflict," "express," and "field"—but all of them work in the same way: Congress enacts a law that imposes restrictions or confers rights on private actors; a state law confers rights or imposes restrictions that conflict with the federal law; and therefore the federal law takes precedence and the state law is preempted.

A recent example [of conflict preemption] is *Mutual Pharmaceutical Co. v. Bartlett*, 570 U.S. 472 (2013). In that case, a federal law enacted under the Commerce Clause regulated manufacturers of generic drugs, prohibiting them from altering either the composition or labeling approved by the Food and Drug Administration. A State's tort law, however, effectively required a manufacturer to supplement the warnings included in the FDA-approved label. We held that the state law was preempted because it imposed a duty that was inconsistent—*i.e.*, in conflict—with federal law.

"Express preemption" operates in essentially the same way, but this is often obscured by the language used by Congress in framing preemption provisions. [I]n *Morales v. Trans World Airlines, Inc.*, 504 U.S. 374 (1992) . . . [t]he Airline Deregulation Act of 1978 lifted prior federal regulations of airlines, and "[t]o ensure that the States would not undo federal deregulation with regulation of their own," the Act provided that "no State or political subdivision thereof

. . . shall enact or enforce any law, rule, regulation, standard, or other provision having the force and effect of law relating to rates, routes, or services of any [covered] air carrier."

This language might appear to operate directly on the States, but it is a mistake to be confused by the way in which a preemption provision is phrased. . . . [I]f we look beyond the phrasing employed in the Airline Deregulation Act's preemption provision, it is clear that this provision operates just like any other federal law with preemptive effect. It confers on private entities (*i.e.,* covered carriers) a federal right to engage in certain conduct subject only to certain (federal) constraints.

"Field preemption" operates in the same way. Field preemption occurs when federal law occupies a "field" of regulation "so comprehensively that it has left no room for supplementary state legislation." In describing field preemption, we have sometimes used the same sort of shorthand employed by Congress in express preemption provisions. See, *e.g., Oneok, Inc. v. Learjet, Inc.,* 575 U.S. ____ (2015) ("Congress has forbidden the State to take action in the *field* that the federal statute pre-empts"). But in substance, field preemption does not involve congressional commands to the States. Instead, like all other forms of preemption, it concerns a clash between a constitutional exercise of Congress's legislative power and conflicting state law.

[I]n *Arizona v. United States*, 567 U.S. 387, [we explained that] federal statutes "provide a full set of standards governing alien registration," [and] we concluded that these laws "reflect[ ] a congressional decision to foreclose any state regulation in the area, even if it is parallel to federal standards." What this means is that the federal registration provisions not only impose federal registration obligations on aliens but also confer a federal right to be free from any other registration requirements.

In sum, regardless of the language sometimes used by Congress and this Court, every form of preemption is based on a federal law that regulates the conduct of private actors, not the States.

[I]t is clear that the PASPA provision prohibiting state authorization of sports gambling is not a preemption provision because there is no way in which this provision can be understood as a regulation of private actors. It certainly does not confer any federal rights on private actors interested in conducting sports gambling operations. (It does not give them a federal right to engage in sports gambling.) Nor does it impose any federal restrictions on private actors. . . . Thus, there is simply no way to understand the provision prohibiting state authorization as anything other than a direct command to the States. And that is exactly what the anticommandeering rule does not allow.

VI

[Justice Alito concluded that PASPA's prohibition of state licensing of sports gambling also violated the anticomandeering principle.] Just as Congress lacks the power to order a state legislature not to enact a law authorizing sports gambling, it may not order a state legislature to refrain from enacting a law licensing sports gambling.

Finally, Justice Alito concluded that the offending provision was not severable from the rest of PAPSA, so that the entire statute, which prohibited states and private parties from sponsoring, operating, or advertising, or promoting sports gambling schemes, was invalid.]

[A concurring opinion by Justice Thomas is omitted.]

[Justice Ginsburg dissented, joined by Justice Sotomayor and in part by Justice Breyer. She argued that the Court should not have struck down two features of PAPSA. The first bans States themselves (or their agencies) from "sponsor[ing], operat[ing], advertis[ing], [or] promot[ing]" sports-gambling schemes. The second stops private parties from "sponsor[ing], operat[ing], advertis[ing], or promot[ing]" sports-gambling schemes if state law authorizes them to do so. "Nothing in these . . . prohibitions commands States to do anything other than desist from conduct federal law proscribes." Justice Breyer agreed with the Court's constitutional analysis but agreed with Justice Ginsburg that parts of the statute should survive.]

Discussion

1. *Severability.* If the Court had struck down the ban on authorization of sports gambling schemes but not any other part of PAPSA, the federal ban on private parties "sponsor[ing], operat[ing], advertis[ing], or promot[ing]" sports-gambling schemes would have remained in place, and the NCAA and the sports leagues would still have been able to enforce it. Thus, the most important practical effect of *Murphy* was Justice Alito's severability holding—that if Congress had known that it could not constitutionally prohibit states from authorizing sports gambling schemes, Congress would not have wanted to leave the general federal ban on sports gambling in place. Do you agree?

2. *Ordering versus forbidding.* The Court argues that, from the standpoint of federalism, there is no difference between ordering a state to pass a particular regulation and forbidding it from passing a regulation. Consider Justice Alito's three justifications for the anticommandeering principle. Are they equally powerful in the context of forbidding a state from passing a law?

When the federal government forbids a state from passing a new law, does it shift additional enforcement costs to the state, or does it simply preserve the regulatory status quo? (What if regulatory costs increase over time? Should we say that the federal government is, in effect, shifting costs to the state?)

What about blurring of lines of responsibility? Does forbidding a state from passing a new law tend to confuse voters about who bears responsibility for the state's failure the law? For example, is it reasonable to think that PAPSA confused New Jersey's voters about the reason why the state hadn't legalized gambling? Why wouldn't New Jersey politicians have incentives to blame the federal government, making clear where the responsibility lay? On the other hand, are the incentives any different in a case in which the federal government requires New Jersey to pass a law? If not, this suggests that the confusion argument is not very strong in either the case of requiring or forbidding.

Perhaps preventing states from changing their laws eliminates a potential source of liberty. On the other hand, does PAPSA limit liberty more than if the federal government had simply directly prohibited gambling?

3. *Anticommandeering and preemption.* This last point suggests that *Murphy* may really be a requirement that federal government use direct regulation (and thus preemption) rather than forbidding states to pass new laws. As long as both states and private parties are prohibited from sponsoring gambling, Alito explains, there is no anticommandeering problem. Why do you think the federal government did not simply preempt state gambling laws and prohibit sports betting nationwide? One possibility is that a single federal rule would have made it more difficult politically to justify the grandfathering provisions for certain states. A second is that the federal government might have wanted to keep sports gambling illegal where bans existed but allow each state to decide on the appropriate penalties and methods of gambling regulation, keeping these questions (and prosecutions) within the state criminal justice system.

Note: Sanctuary Cities and Federalism

New federalism problems have arisen from the Trump Adminstration's attacks on "sanctuary cities." The term has no settled legal meaning. Key debates concern whether states and municipalities will cooperate with federal immigration officials in identifying, detaining, and delivering persons suspected of being undocumented aliens to federal officials.

An ICE detainer — or "immigration hold" — is an enforcement tool used by U.S. Immigration and Customs Enforcement (ICE). An ICE civil detainer request asks a local law enforcement agency to continue to hold an inmate who is in a local jail because of actual or suspected violations of state criminal laws for up to 48 hours after his or her scheduled release so that ICE can determine if it wants to take that individual into ICE custody.

Largely because of federalism doctrines such as *Printz v. United States*, ICE civil detainer requests are voluntary and local governments are not required to honor them. *See also Morales v. Chadbourne*, 793 F.3d 208, 215–217 (1st Cir. 2015) (holding that it is a violation of the Fourth Amendment for local jurisdictions to hold suspected or actual removable aliens in response to civil detainer requests because civil detainer requests are often not supported by an individualized determination of probable cause that a crime has been committed.) ICE does not reimburse local jurisdictions for the cost of detaining individuals in response to a civil detainer request and it does not indemnify local jurisdictions for the potential liability they could face for related Fourth Amendment violations.

A 1996 law, 8 U.S.C. § 1373, provides that a "State, or local government entity or official may not prohibit, or in any way restrict, any government entity or official from sending to, or receiving from, the Immigration and Naturalization Service information regarding the citizenship or immigration status, lawful or unlawful, of any individual." ICE is the successor of the Immigration and Naturalization Service. Is § 1373 consistent with the Tenth Amendment doctrines enunciated in *New York*, *Printz*, and *Murphy?* Could one read § 1373 narrowly to avoid constitutional problems?

As a presidential candidate, Donald Trump spoke out against sanctuary cities, and promised that he would end them. Shortly after taking office, on January 25, 2017, President Trump issued Executive Order No. 13768, "Enhancing Public Safety in the Interior of the United States." 82 Fed. Reg. 8799 (Jan. 25, 2017). Section 1 of the order reads, in part, "Sanctuary jurisdictions across the United States willfully violate Federal law in an attempt to shield aliens from removal from the United States." Section 2 states that the policy of the executive branch is to "[e]nsure that jurisdictions that fail to comply with applicable Federal law do not receive Federal funds, except as mandated by law."

Section 9(a) of the Executive Order restricts federal grants going to "sanctuary jurisdictions." It provides:

> In furtherance of this policy, the Attorney General and the Secretary [of Homeland Security], in their discretion and to the extent consistent with law, shall ensure that jurisdictions that willfully refuse to comply with 8 U.S.C. 1373 (sanctuary jurisdictions) are not eligible to receive Federal grants, except as deemed necessary for law enforcement purposes by the Attorney General or the Secretary. The Secretary has the authority to designate, in his discretion and to the extent consistent with law, a jurisdiction as a sanctuary jurisdiction. The Attorney General shall take appropriate enforcement action against any entity that violates 8 U.S.C. 1373, or which has in effect a statute, policy, or practice that prevents or hinders the enforcement of Federal law.

The Executive Order does not define "sanctuary jurisdiction" nor does it define what constitutes "willfully refus[ing] to comply with" § 1373. Section 1373, in turn, makes no mention of federal funds; it does not condition receipt of funds on compliance and it does not authorize withholding funds for violation.

Is the Executive Order consistent with the Constitution? Consider the following questions:

(1) Does the President have authority to withhold federal funds to enforce § 1373 if Congress has not explicitly authorized him to do so?

(2) Assuming that the President can condition receipt of federal funds on compliance with § 1373, is the resulting restriction on federal funds beyond federal powers under *South Dakota v. Dole* and *NFIB v. Sebelius?*

The Executive Order threatens to remove funding for all federal grants except funds "deemed necessary for law enforcement purposes." That means that the federal grants threatened concern those not deemed necessary for law enforcement purposes. Is there a sufficient nexus between the President's requirement and the funds that the President threatens to withhold? If there is a sufficient nexus, is the amount of federal funding (or the percentage of a state's or municipality's budget) withheld sufficiently large to be coercive under *Sebelius*?

For further discussion, see City and County Of San Francisco v. Trump, 897 F.3d 1225 (9th Cir. 2018)(holding that the Executive Order was not authorized by Congress and therefore violated separation of powers); City of Seattle v. Trump, 250 F.Supp.3d 497 (W.D. Wash. 2017) (denying government motion to dismiss); City of Philadelphia v. Sessions, 280 F.Supp.3d 579 (E.D. Pa. 2018) (holding that the attempt to withhold federal grants was arbitrary and capricious and that § 1373 was unconstitutional under Murphy v. NCAA); see also United States v. California, 921 F.3d 865 (9th Cir. 2019) (upholding a California immigration law from a federal preemption challenge and invoking anti-commandeering principles); City of Los Angeles v. Barr, 2019 WL 3049129 (9th Cir. 2019) (upholding competitive grant program that awards extra points to applicants who agree to cooperate with federal officials on immigration enforcement).

Insert the following on p. 867 before subsection B:

Note: Congressional Oversight in the Trump Presidency

In January 2019, Democrats gained control of the House of Representatives. Under the previous Republican majority, there was relatively little oversight or investigation into President Trump's many scandals. Democrats signaled that they were ready to make up for lost time. They began to issue multiple requests for documents and testimony.

President Trump offered a characteristically aggressive response: " 'We're fighting all the subpoenas,' Mr. Trump told reporters outside the White House. 'These aren't, like, impartial people. The Democrats are trying to win 2020.' "[32]

Thus began a series of controversies in which House Democrats requested material and testimony, and the White House refused. We can divide the controversies into three different groups of issues.

1. *Assertions of executive privilege and categorical "immunity" with respect to Administration documents and the testimony of Administration officials.* President Trump has repeatedly asserted executive privilege with respect to document requests from Congress, including with respect to documents previously made available to Special Counsel Robert Mueller (who was part of the Executive Branch).

---

32. Charlie Savage, Trump Vows Stonewall of 'All' House Subpoenas, Setting Up Fight Over Powers, New York Times, April 24, 2019, https://www.nytimes.com/2019/04/24/us/politics/donald-trump-subpoenas.html

President Trump has also repeatedly refused to allow current and former Administration officials to testify before Congress. Executive privilege allows the President to prevent senior advisors who work with and advise him every day from disclosing their conversations and interactions with him. In order to protect that privilege, the executive branch has historically asserted testimonial immunity with respect to the President's close advisors who regularly meet with and advise him. Moreover, it has also asserted this immunity with respect to former officials. These claims of testimonial immunity have been executive branch positions in both Democratic and Republican Administrations.

However, the President does not have effective control over former officials, and it is up to them to decide whether to testify, and, if so, whether to assert the privilege (or a form of "immunity" from testimony).[33] They may do so out of their loyalty to the President for whom they served, in order to protect the institution of the Presidency, because of their ethical obligations as attorneys, or for other political or personal reasons.

The only judicial decision squarely on point rejects the Executive branch's position on testimonial immunity. In Comm. on Judiciary, U.S. House of Representatives v. Miers, 558 F. Supp. 2d 53, 100–02 (D.D.C. 2008) the district court rejected absolute immunity for former senior presidential advisors. The case involved Harriet Miers, who at that time was a former White House Counsel to President George W. Bush. The district court agreed that immunity might be appropriate in cases "where national security or foreign affairs form the basis for the Executive's assertion of privilege." Senior advisors could also "assert executive privilege in response to any specific questions posed by the Committee." The district court, however, rejected a general immunity from having to testify:

> There are powerful reasons supporting the rejection of absolute immunity as asserted by the Executive here. If the Court held otherwise, the presumptive presidential privilege could be transformed into an absolute privilege and Congress's legitimate interest in inquiry could be easily thwarted. . . . [I]f the Executive's absolute immunity argument were to prevail, Congress could be left with no recourse to obtain information that is plainly not subject to any colorable claim of executive privilege. . . . Clear precedent and persuasive policy reasons confirm that the Executive cannot be the judge of its own privilege . . . Ms. Miers is not excused from compliance with the Committee's subpoena by virtue of a claim of executive privilege that may ultimately be made. Instead, she must appear before the Committee to provide testimony, and invoke executive privilege where appropriate.

The Executive Branch has not accepted the *Miers* decision as a correct statement of the law.

33. See Marty Lederman, What Is a Private Citizen to Do (When Caught in the Middle of an Interbranch Dispute)?, Balkinization, July 11, 2007, https://balkin.blogspot.com/2007/07/whatis-private-citizen-to-do-when.html

President Trump has also begun to assert the privilege beyond the smaller circle of senior advisors who interact with and advise the President every day.[34] In addition, the Trump Administration has been asserting a prophylactic claim of executive privilege with respect to large classes of documents.[35]

Beyond the central precedent of United States v. Nixon, which held that executive privilege must yield to "the fundamental demands of due process of law in the fair administration of justice," there is very little case law on the scope of executive privilege. (See *Miers, supra.*) A large number of opinions have been produced not by the courts but by the Justice Department's Office of Legal Counsel, and therefore are understandably sympathetic to the position of the President. Whatever one thinks the actual scope of executive privilege should be, the President has institutional incentives to claim a far broader privilege in conflicts with Congress and the courts.

One reason for the lack of case law is the practical problem of enforcement. Congress can issue a subpoena for documents or testimony. But if the President asserts executive privilege, Congress's options are limited.

First, Congress can vote (or threaten to vote) government officials in contempt for failing to appear, or for refusing to produce requested documents. For example, a Republican-controlled House held Attorney General Eric Holder in criminal and civil contempt in 2012 in a dispute over document production in the House's investigation of the Fast and Furious scandal involving the Bureau of Alcohol, Tobacco, and Firearms. The contempt citation, however, was practically ineffective: the document production issues were not resolved until the spring of 2019, long after President Obama left office.

That is because Congress has few ways of enforcing its orders. Congress has inherent powers to enforce its orders through contempt proceedings, arrest and imprisonment, but it has chosen not to use them for close to a century. See McGrain v. Daugherty, 273 U.S. 135 (1927)(upholding Congress's power to arrest and detain a witness in a Congressional investigation of antitrust policy.); Anderson v. Dunn, 19 U.S. (6 Wheat.) 204 (1821)(holding that Congress has the power to punish for contempt). Because Congress does not use its own contempt powers, Congress has to rely on criminal or civil proceedings.

Criminal proceedings require Congress to refer a matter to a U.S. Attorney. But the U.S. Attorney works for the Justice Department, which is part of the Executive Branch. The usual policy of the Justice Department is to refuse to bring criminal contempt proceedings against a member of the Executive Branch who is relying upon a claim of privilege or immunity that the President and DOJ

---

34. See, e.g., Jacqueline Thomsen, White House sought to assert executive privilege in Kobach interview on census citizenship question, Cummings says, The Hill, June 7, 2019,https://thehill.com/regulation/court-battles/447510-white-house-sought-to-assert-executive-privilege-in-kobach-interview;RyanGoodmanandJohnT.Nelson,AnnieDonaldsonisNotthePresident's"AlterEgo",JustSecurity, June 24, 2019 https://www.justsecurity.org/64681/annie-donaldson-is-not-the-presidents-alter-ego/

35. See Jonathan Shaub, The Prophylactic Executive Privilege, Lawfare, June 14, 2019, https://www.lawfareblog.com/prophylactic-executive-privilege

have approved. For example, after the House held Attorney General Eric Holder in contempt in 2012, the Justice Department refused to prosecute.

That leaves civil proceedings. Congress can go to federal court to enforce its orders. But court proceedings generally take a great deal of time — sometimes many years. By the time the appeals process is exhausted, the Administration may be out of office — or Congress held by a different party.

As a result, most disputes over executive privilege are resolved by negotiations between the two branches, which usually come to some sort of accommodation. Because Congress and the President regularly need to cooperate on many topics and at many levels, there are reasons for each to accommodate the other. Each also has its own balance of considerations. The Executive branch has to balance concerns about bad publicity (i.e., that it is hiding something illegal or embarrassing), and about the possibility of congressional payback in other contexts, against the Executive branch's interests in protecting the confidentiality of its operations over the long run. Conversely, Congress has to balance its desire for information against its own concerns about bad publicity, as well as the possibility that negotiations will break down and Congress must go to the courts and face a protracted struggle.

In the Trump Administration, the Executive Branch has somewhat fewer incentives for cooperation than usual. There is very little that Trump wants from a Democratic House and little to gain politically from cooperating with them. Accordingly, President Trump has made fairly broad assertions of privilege and attempted to delay resolution of disputes with Congress, cooperating only when necessary. By acting intransigently on multiple fronts, he may be able to wear down Congress. Even if many of his claims of executive privilege and testimonial immunity are overblown, they simply add to Congress's work in having to deal with them.

To be sure, Congress can threaten to impeach the President for his refusals. It can also begin impeachment proceedings and use them to investigate the President. There is a plausible argument that executive privilege must yield, or that its scope is far narrower, when Congress is investigating articles of impeachment. Otherwise, the President would truly be beyond investigation and accountability.

However, impeachment proceedings are the strongest possible weapon in Congress's arsenal — a bit like a nuclear device. They also may have unpredictable political effects for the party that controls the House. That is especially so because the Senate, which is controlled by the President's allies, is unlikely to convict and remove him before the 2020 elections. In May 2019, House Speaker Nancy Pelosi speculated that Trump's intransigence is a ploy: "Trump is goading us to impeach him . . . he knows that it would be very divisive in the country, but he doesn't really care. He just wants to solidify his base."[36] If Democrats are not interested in impeaching a President who stonewalls them repeatedly, their options for compliance become quite limited. They can try to leverage things that the President wants or needs from House Democrats. But because the

---

36. Clare Foran, Ashley Killough and Sunlen Serfaty, Nancy Pelosi: 'Trump is goading us to impeach him', CNN, May 7, 2019, https://www.cnn.com/2019/05/07/politics/pelosi-impeachment-trump-congress/index.html

Republican Party controls the Senate, the House has no control over executive branch appointments and judgeships.

Although disputes and bargaining between the branches has been commonplace. President Trump's blanket assertion that he will fight *all* congressional requests for documents and testimony is unprecedented in American history. If the judiciary cannot respond quickly, what role should norms and conventions play in characterizing what is happening? In restraining the political branches?[37] What should the other participants do if one of the participants refuses to accept their understanding of the existing norms?

Suppose you think that Trump's position is inconsistent with existing norms and conventions about how the two parties should bargain in disputes about Congressional oversight. Will norm-breaking have any long term effects, or do you predict that things will snap back to normal in the next presidency?

2. *Documents from third parties and third party witnesses unconnected to the Administration.* Congress has also sought documents from third parties who are not former senior advisors to the President. Executive privilege generally does not apply in these cases. Nevertheless, the Trump Administration has sought to block Congress from reviewing them. In Trump v. Committee On Oversight And Reform Of The U.S. House Of Representatives, 2019 WL 2171378 (D.D.C. 2019), the Trump Administration sought to quash a Congressional subpoena for financial documents from Mazars USA LLP, a firm that has provided accounting services to President Trump. The subpoena called for Mazars to produce financial records and other documents relating to President Trump personally as well as various associated businesses and entities dating back to 2011. The House issued the subpoena after the President's former lawyer and confidant, Michael Cohen, testified before the House Oversight Committee that the President would routinely diminish or inflate the estimated value of his assets and liabilities on financial statements, depending on the purpose for which a statement was needed.

President Trump argued that the Mazars subpoena exceeded Congress's power to conduct investigations, because there was no legitimate legislative purpose for the subpoena. The Oversight Committee's true motive, the President argued, was to collect personal information about him solely for political advantage.

The Supreme Court has held that Congress has the power to conduct investigations "as an attribute of the power to legislate." McGrain v. Daugherty, 273 U.S. 135, 161 (1927). "It was so regarded in the British Parliament and in the colonial Legislatures before the American Revolution, and a like view has prevailed and been carried into effect in both houses of Congress and in most of the state Legislatures." Id. Congress has the power "by itself or through its committees, to investigate matters and conditions relating to contemplated legislation." Quinn v. United States, 349 U.S. 155, 160 (1955). Congress also has the power

---

37. On the role of norms in executive branch practice, see Daphna Renan, Presidential Norms and Article II, 131 Harv. L. Rev. 2187 (2018). On the role of norms more generally in sustaining the rule of law, see Tara Leigh Grove, The Origins (and Fragility) of Judicial Independence, 71 Vand. L. Rev. 465 (2018).

to inform itself about facts and circumstances in furtherance of its investigative functions. And it has a broader "informing function" that extends at the very least to "prob[ing] into departments of the Federal Government to expose corruption, inefficiency or waste." Watkins v. United States, 354 U.S. 178, 187 (1957).

In *Watkins*, the Supreme Court reversed a conviction for contempt of Congress when Watkins appeared before the House Committee on Un-American Activities and refused to answer questions about who he believed was a member of the Communist Party. The Court held that the conviction violated Due Process because the defendant did not obtain fair notice as to why the questions he was being asked were pertinent to the subject of the committee's investigation. The Court described Congress's power of investigation this way:

> The power of the Congress to conduct investigations is inherent in the legislative process. That power is broad. It encompasses inquiries concerning the administration of existing laws as well as proposed or possibly needed statutes. It includes surveys of defects in our social, economic or political system for the purpose of enabling the Congress to remedy them. It comprehends probes into departments of the Federal Government to expose corruption, inefficiency or waste. But, broad as is this power of inquiry, it is not unlimited. There is no general authority to expose the private affairs of individuals without justification in terms of the functions of the Congress. . . . Nor is the Congress a law enforcement or trial agency. These are functions of the executive and judicial departments of government. No inquiry is an end in itself; it must be related to, and in furtherance of, a legitimate task of the Congress. Investigations conducted solely for the personal aggrandizement of the investigators or to "punish" those investigated are indefensible. . . .
>
> We have no doubt that there is no congressional power to expose for the sake of exposure. The public is, of course, entitled to be informed concerning the workings of its government. That cannot be inflated into a general power to expose where the predominant result can only be an invasion of the private rights of individuals. But a solution to our problem is not to be found in testing the motives of committee members for this purpose. Such is not our function. Their motives alone would not vitiate an investigation which had been instituted by a House of Congress if that assembly's legislative purpose is being served.

Id. at 187, 200. In *McGrain v. Daugherty,* the Supreme Court held that if the subject of a Congressional investigation appears to be related to possible legislation, "the presumption should be indulged that this was the real object." Although Congress may state the purposes of its investigation officially, such an official statement is not required.

Applying these precedents, the District Court rejected the President's challenge. It held that although the relevant committee did not pass a resolution specifying the purposes of its investigation, it was easy to recognize those legislative purposes: "Congress reasonably might consider those documents in connection with deciding whether to legislate on federal ethics laws and regulations . . . [T]here can be little doubt that Congress's interest in the accuracy of the President's financial disclosures falls within the legislative sphere." The court also pointed out that Congress might be interested in discovering "whether the

President is abiding by the Foreign Emoluments Clause," which can be a subject of congressional action or legislation. Congress might also be interested in "whether the President has any conflicts of interest," because Congress regulates government ethics. "Finally, a congressional investigation into 'illegal conduct before and during [the President's] tenure in office,' . . . fits comfortably within the broad scope of Congress's investigative powers. At a minimum, such an investigation is justified based on Congress's 'informing function,' that is, its power 'to inquire into and publicize corruption.'" [*Watkins*]

The court added: "It is simply not fathomable that a Constitution that grants Congress the power to remove a President for reasons including criminal behavior would deny Congress the power to investigate him for unlawful conduct—past or present—even without formally opening an impeachment inquiry." Moreover, "[t]wice in the last 50 years Congress has investigated a sitting President for alleged law violations, before initiating impeachment proceedings. It did so in 1973 by establishing the Senate Select Committee on Presidential Campaign Activities, better known as the Watergate Committee, and then did so again in 1995 by establishing the Special Committee to Investigate Whitewater Development Corporation and Related Matters. . . . Congress plainly views itself as having sweeping authority to investigate illegal conduct of a President, before and after taking office. This court is not prepared to roll back the tide of history."

Why has the Supreme Court refused to look too closely into legislators' motives in deciding whether an investigation is within Congress' powers? Note that during the Obama Administration, the Republican-controlled House of Representatives engaged in six different lengthy investigations of a 2012 terrorist attack on the American government facilities in Benghazi, Libya, which resulted in the deaths of four Americans. (The Republican-controlled Senate engaged in two separate investigations of its own). The hearings were widely touted on Fox News and other conservative media as evidence of a cover up of a nefarious conspiracy, which was about to be revealed, but which was never found. Critics charged that the real purpose of these investigations was to cast the Obama Administration as unpatriotic and to undermine Secretary of State Hillary Clinton's chances at running for president in 2016. Indeed, one of the side effects of the investigation was to provide additional attention to the fact that Secretary Clinton had used a private e-mail server during her time in office. This revelation became an important issue in the 2016 elections.

What are the advantages and disadvantages of the Supreme Court's current test? Why should courts refuse to look beyond Congress's public articulation of the reasons for its investigations? Why should courts refuse to look into motives? How is the Court's rule of deference in *Watkins* and other cases similar to or different from the deference it afforded the President in the travel ban case, *Hawaii v. Trump*?

3. *The President's tax returns.* In defiance of long-standing political conventions, President Trump famously refused to disclose his tax returns during the 2016 campaign, offering various excuses for why he was not yet able to do so. After the election, he announced that he would not release them. His refusal to make his tax returns public infuriated his political opponents, who sought various ways to discover what was in them.

Federal law treats federal tax returns as confidential, and the Treasury Department generally may not disclose them to the public or to other parties. 26 U.S.C. §§ 6103(a), 7213(a). However, there are exceptions for authorized disclosures. One such disclosure appears in 26 U.S.C. § 6103(f)(1), which provides that "Upon written request from the chairman of the Committee on Ways and Means of the House of Representatives, the chairman of the Committee on Finance of the Senate, or the chairman of the Joint Committee on Taxation, the Secretary [of the Treasury] shall furnish such committee with any return or return information specified in such request, except that any return or return information which can be associated with, or otherwise identify, directly or indirectly, a particular taxpayer shall be furnished to such committee only when sitting in closed executive session unless such taxpayer otherwise consents in writing to such disclosure." Subsection (f)(4)(A) authorizes the House Ways and Means Committee and the Senate Finance Committee — unlike other committees — to share such information with the full House or Senate, thereby effectively making it public.

On April 3, 2019, the Chairman of the House Committee on Ways and Means, Representative Richard Neal, requested the last six years of President Trump's individual tax returns, and those of eight associated business entities, as well as the audit histories and work papers associated with each return. Chairman Neal explained the reason for his request as follows:

> Consistent with its authority, the Committee is considering legislative proposals and conducting oversight related to our Federal tax laws, including, but not limited to, the extent to which the IRS audits and enforces the Federal tax laws against a President. Under the Internal Revenue Manual, individual income tax returns of a President are subject to mandatory examination, but this practice is IRS policy and not codified in the Federal tax laws. It is necessary for the Committee to determine the scope of any such examination and whether it includes a review of underlying business activities required to be reported on the individual income tax return.

Treasury Secretary Steven Mnuchin refused to release the returns, and on June 13, 2019, the Office of Legal Counsel issued an opinion.[38] The OLC opinion argued that

> The text of section 6103(f). . . . does not require the Committee to state any purpose for its request. But Congress could not constitutionally confer upon the Committee the right to compel the Executive Branch to disclose confidential information without a legitimate legislative purpose. Under the facts and circumstances, the Secretary of the Treasury reasonably and correctly concluded that the Committee's asserted interest in reviewing the Internal Revenue Service's audits of presidential returns was pretextual and that its true aim was to make the President's tax returns public, which is not a legitimate legislative purpose.
>
> . . .

---

38. Congressional Committee's Request for the President's Tax Returns Under 26 U.S.C. § 6103(f), Office of Legal Counsel (June 13, 2019), https://www.justice.gov/olc/file/1173756/download

During the prior Congress, Chairman Neal, who was then the Committee's Ranking Member, repeatedly urged the Committee to invoke section 6103(f) to make the President's tax returns "available to the public," declaring that "Committee Democrats remain steadfast in [their] pursuit to have [President Trump's] individual tax returns disclosed to the public." . . . Before the midterm elections, Chairman Neal (as well as other members of his party) promised that, if they won a majority in the House, then the Chairman would wield his authority to demand the President's tax returns.

. . . .

While the Executive Branch should accord due deference and respect to a committee's request, the Committee's stated purpose in the April 3 letter blinks reality. It is pretextual. No one could reasonably believe that the Committee seeks six years of President Trump's tax returns because of a newly discovered interest in legislating on the presidential-audit process. The Committee's request reflects the next assay in a long-standing political battle over the President's tax returns. Consistent with their long-held views, Chairman Neal and other majority members have invoked the Committee's authority to obtain and publish these returns. Recognizing that the Committee may not pursue exposure for exposure's sake, however, the Committee has devised an alternative reason for the request.

. . . When faced with a congressional request for confidential taxpayer information, must the Secretary close his eyes and blindly accept a pretextual justification for that request? Or must the Secretary implement the statute in a manner faithful to constitutional limitations? We believe that the Executive's duty to "take Care that the Laws be faithfully executed," U.S. Const. art. II, § 3, permits only one answer. Where, as here, there is reason to doubt the Committee's asserted legislative purpose, Treasury may examine the objective fit between that purpose and the information sought, as well as any other evidence that may bear upon the Committee's true objective. In doing so, Treasury acts as part of a politically accountable branch with a constitutional duty to resist legislative intrusions upon executive power and therefore does not act under the same institutional constraints as the Judiciary. Here, because the Committee lacked a legitimate legislative purpose, its request did not qualify for the statutory exception to taxpayer confidentiality, and the law required Treasury to deny that request.

Is the OLC's argument consistent with *Watkins*? Compare the reasoning in *Hawaii v. Trump*. Should courts treat accusations of pretextual reasoning by the Executive and the Legislative branches differently? Why or why not?

Note the OLC's argument that it "does not act under the same institutional constraints as the Judiciary." Because both Congress and the Executive are elected branches, they are in a different position than an unelected judiciary. But if the case goes before the federal judiciary, won't the judiciary have to work within these institutional constraints in deciding whether or not to defer to Congress and uphold Chairman Neal's request?

In its opinion, the OLC claimed that the real reasons for the request are to discover and expose to the public Trump's potential financial conflicts of interest and ties to foreign nations, and, in particular, to assess what "the Russians have on Donald Trump politically, personally, [and] financially" and to "help the American people better understand the extent of Trump's financial ties to Putin's

Russia" (quoting House members). If the OLC is right that those are the real, or at least the primary, reasons for the House's request, why wouldn't those reasons be sufficient to justify the disclosure?

Insert on p. 957 before Note: The Power to Wage War

Note: The Border Wall and National Emergencies

In 2016 Donald Trump campaigned on building a border wall with Mexico, which, he originally promised, Mexico would pay for. Once in office, President Trump turned to Congress to fund the wall. During the first two years of his Administration, he had only limited success, even though his party controlled both Houses of Congress. In December of 2018, a month before the Democrats were scheduled to take control of the House of Representatives, the President vetoed an appropriations bill because it did not contain sufficient funding for a border wall. The President sought 5.7 billion dollars for the construction of a steel barrier for the Southwest border, and refused to sign a new bill funding the government until Congress agreed.

The result was the longest partial shutdown of the federal government in U.S. history, lasting 35 days. The shutdown ended when the President and Congress agreed to enact the Consolidated Appropriations Act of 2019 ("CAA"), which provided $ 1.375 billion for new border fencing in the Rio Grande Valley — several billion dollars short of what the President had asked for in his budget request. See Pub. L. No. 116-6 (2019). Throughout the shutdown, the President and his political allies debated whether to resolve the standoff by declaring a national emergency that would allow the President to use various funds designed for emergency situations.

On February 15, 2019, the same day he signed the CAA into law, President Trump declared that "a national emergency exists at the southern border of the United States." Proclamation No. 9844, 84 Fed. Reg. 4949 (Feb. 15, 2019) ("National Emergency Declaration"). The declaration stated:

> The current situation at the southern border presents a border security and humanitarian crisis that threatens core national security interests and constitutes a national emergency. The southern border is a major entry point for criminals, gang members, and illicit narcotics. The problem of large-scale unlawful migration through the southern border is long-standing, and despite the executive branch's exercise of existing statutory authorities, the situation has worsened in certain respects in recent years. In particular, recent years have seen sharp increases in the number of family units entering and seeking entry to the United States and an inability to provide detention space for many of these aliens while their removal proceedings are pending. If not detained, such aliens are often released into the country and are often difficult to remove from the United States because they fail to appear for hearings, do not comply with orders of removal, or are otherwise difficult to locate. In response to the directive in my April 4, 2018, memorandum and subsequent

requests for support by the Secretary of Homeland Security, the Department of
Defense has provided support and resources to the Department of Homeland
Security at the southern border. Because of the gravity of the current emergency
situation, it is necessary for the Armed Forces to provide additional support to
address the crisis.

In declaring a national emergency, the President invoked his authority under
the National Emergencies Act ("NEA"), Pub. L. 94–412, 90 Stat. 1255 (1976)
(codified as amended at 50 U.S.C. §§ 1601–1651). Under the NEA, once the
President "specifically declares a national emergency," the President may exercise emergency powers that have been authorized by Congress in other federal
statutes. 50 U.S.C. § 1621. In order to exercise a statutory emergency power, the
President must first specify the power or authority under which the President or
other officers will act, "either in the declaration of a national emergency, or by
one or more contemporaneous or subsequent Executive orders published in the
Federal Register and transmitted to the Congress." Id. § 1631. Section 1622 then
establishes a procedure for Congress to terminate any declared national emergency through a joint resolution, which is subject to a presidential veto.

In response, on March 14, Congress passed a joint resolution to terminate the
President's declaration of a national emergency. See H.R.J. Res. 46, 116th Cong.
(2019). The President vetoed Congress's joint resolution on March 15, 2019.
The House voted 248-181 to override the President's veto, falling short of the
required two-thirds majority.

As originally drafted, §1622 of the NEA allowed Congress to terminate any
declared national emergency by a joint resolution without the need for a presidential signature. This meant that Congress could stop the President from using
his or her emergency powers without being subject to a presidential veto. The
NEA did not define the term "national emergency" because it was assumed that
Congress would exercise oversight and act as a check on the President's use
of emergency powers. However, in 1983, the Supreme Court decided INS v.
Chadha, 462 U.S. 919 (1983) (Casebook p. 913), which held that the President
must have the power to approve or veto congressional acts that have the force of
law. Two years later, Congress amended the NEA to reflect that the joint resolution must be "enacted into law" to terminate a President's declared emergency.
See Pub. L. No. 99-93, § 801(1)(A), 99 Stat. 405, 448 (1985).

The Trump Administration announced plans to cobble together approximately
8.1 billion dollars for wall construction from a variety of sources. The Trump
Administration has pointed to three major sources of funding, on top of the
$ 1.375 billion Congress appropriated through the CAA, to build the border wall.
See President Donald J. Trump's Border Security Victory, White House (Feb.
15, 2019), ECF No. 36-7, https://www.whitehouse.gov/briefingsstatements/
president-donald-j-trumps-border-security-victory/.

First, the Administration announced that it planned to use $ 601 million from
the Treasury Forfeiture Fund.

Second, the Administration sought to use up to $ 3.6 billion reallocated
from Department of Defense military construction projects under 10 U.S.C.

§ 2808(a). Upon a declaration of a national emergency "that requires the use of armed forces," the Secretary of Defense "may authorize the Secretaries of the military departments to undertake military construction projects, not otherwise authorized by law that are necessary to support such use of the armed forces." 10 U.S.C. § 2808(a). This is the only planned use of funds that depends upon President Trump's declaration of a national emergency.

Third, the Administration sought to "reprogram," (i.e., move) up to $ 2.5 billion in funds appropriated for the Department of Defense to the Department of Homeland Security for border construction, using its authority under 10 U.S.C. § 284.

Several lawsuits have challenged the President's use of 10 U.S.C. §§ 2808, 284, and section 8005 of the NDAA, on the ground that these statutes do not authorize the use of funds for building a border wall and that therefore the Administration's planned spending is *ultra vires*, or without legal authority. Some of the suits have also alleged that such spending without a valid appropriation violates the Constitution's Appropriations Clause.

In U.S. House Of Representatives v. Mnuchin, 2019 WL 2343015 (D.D.C. 2019), the district court held that the House of Representatives did not have standing to challenge the President's use of Congress's appropriated funds.

In Sierra Club v. Trump, 2019 WL 2247689 (N.D. Calif. 2019), the district court held that because of the construction's environmental impact, the Sierra Club had standing to challenge the border wall construction. The district court preliminarily enjoined the use of reprogrammed funds under 10 U.S.C. §284 on the grounds that the Administration had not met the legal preconditions for such a transfer. Section 8005 of Pub. L. No. 115-245 authorizes the Secretary to transfer funds pursuant to § 284 only to address "unforeseen military requirement[s]," and only for items of expenditure not previously "denied by the Congress." The district court found that the need to build a wall for counter-narcotics purposes (which was the predicate for the § 284 spending) was anything but "unforeseen," and that Congress had "denied" the "item for which funds are requested" when it refused to appropriate the funds President Trump had specifically requested for the "wall."

A panel of the 9th Circuit, passing on the issues in the context of a petition for a stay, agreed with the District Court by a 2-1 vote. Sierra Club v. Trump, 2019 WL 2865491 (9th Cir. 2019). The Ninth Circuit panel also concluded that "Defendants' attempt to reprogram and spend these funds . . . violates the Appropriations Clause and intrudes on Congress's exclusive power of the purse, for it would cause funds to be 'drawn from the Treasury' not 'in Consequence of Appropriations made by Law.' U.S. Const. art. I, § 9, cl. 7."

Judge Smith, dissenting, argued that the plaintiffs lacked standing under the Administrative Procedure Act. He also argued that there was no constitutional issue in the case. There was merely a statutory claim that the President had acted *ultra vires*: "The majority here takes an uncharted and risky approach — turning every question of whether an executive officer exceeded a statutory grant of power into a constitutional issue." Relying on Dalton v. Specter, 511 U.S. 462 (1994), Judge Smith explained "that cases such as Youngstown Sheet & Tube Co. v. Sawyer,

343 U.S. 579 (1952) involve constitutional violations, because '[t]he only basis of authority asserted was the [executive's] inherent constitutional power.' In those instances, 'the case necessarily turned on whether the Constitution authorized the [executive's] actions,' only '[b]ecause no statutory authority was claimed.' " In this case, by contrast, the Trump Administration was relying on an interpretation of section 8005, so there was no independent constitutional issue.

A few weeks after the 9th Circuit decision, the Supreme Court, by a vote of 5-4, granted a stay of the district court's injunction, explaining "that the Government has made a sufficient showing at this stage that the plaintiffs have no cause of action to obtain review of the Acting Secretary's compliance with Section 8005." Trump v. Sierra Club, 588 U.S. __ (2019). This stay allowed the reprogramming of funds (and the construction of the border wall) to go forward. Justices Ginsburg, Sotomayor, and Kagan dissented, with Justice Breyer concurring in part and dissenting in part.

Note that none of these cases have yet addressed the second category of expenditures under section 2808(a), which depends upon the President's "national emergency" declaration.

Discussion

1. It is estimated that the President has 123 different statutory powers available upon declaration of a national emergency. See A Guide to Emergency Powers and Their Use, Brennan Ctr. for Justice (2019), www.brennancenter.org/sites/default/files/legislation/Emergency%20Powers_Printv2.pdf. In the four decades since Congress enacted the NEA, presidents have declared almost sixty national emergencies. See Declared National Emergencies Under the National Emergencies Act, 1978-2018, Brennan Ctr. for Justice (2019), https://www.brennancenter.org/sites/default/files/analysis/NEA%20Declarations.pdf. Many of these declarations seem to have little to do with emergency in the ordinary sense of the word. They concern export controls, freezing assets of foreign entities, and prohibitions on doing business with certain countries. Moreover, many of these states of emergency have continued for decades without being terminated. The declaration of a state of emergency following the September 11, 2001 terrorist attacks is still in force, for example.

Is there a problem with using the term "emergency" to legitimate so many different kinds of grants of executive power? Is there a problem with keeping these "emergencies" in force for long periods of time? What are the potential risks involved in allowing the President to declare states of emergency so easily? Does it matter that, in contrast to the recent controversy over expenditures to build the "wall," Congress has effectively acquiesced in virtually all of these previous emergency declarations (in the sense of not raising any objections), even as the emergencies extend for decades?

2. Congress's attempt to terminate President Trump's emergency declaration via a joint resolution was the first attempt in the NEA's history. In general Congress allows the President considerable leeway in declaring emergencies. This case was exceptional, and the most likely reason is that many members of Congress did not think that President Trump was responding to a genuine emergency. Moreover, as the shutdown dragged on, it was widely understood—and indeed, publicly stated by Trump and his supporters—that the President was

considering an emergency declaration to get around Congress's refusal to fund a border wall. However, because the President could veto the joint resolution and had enough supporters in Congress to sustain the veto, he was able to evade termination of the emergency.

3. Should the Court revisit *Chadha* in light of this example? Should Congress repeal its grants of emergency power on the ground that they give the President too much power? Should Congress try to define national emergency narrowly in the NEA? Can you think of other ways to design a system of emergency powers that would be more effective in limiting potential abuse by the President?

Add the following at the end of p. 1012, immediately before Note: Presidential Selection:

Note: The Emoluments Clauses

President Donald Trump is unique among modern American presidents for the vast financial holdings he had accumulated at the time he assumed office. In contrast to other modern chief executives such as Barack Obama, most of his wealth has not been in the form of holdings of securities and mutual funds, which could, in theory, be converted into holdings placed in a blind trust. Instead, much of President Trump's wealth comes from his leadership of a family business and its various real estate holdings and licensing deals around the globe.

Traditionally, incoming presidents have worked with ethics counsels to place their assets in a blind trust or to otherwise minimize conflicts of interest during the period they are in office. Shortly after the 2016 election, Trump brushed aside concerns about conflicts of interest, stating that "the law is totally on my side, meaning, the president can't have a conflict of interest."[39] Nevertheless, on January 11, 2017, President Trump promised to distance himself from his businesses, and to hand over operations to his two sons (although he would retain ownership); he also promised that the Trump Organization would not engage in any new deals in foreign countries while he was in office. Even so, his business affairs continue to be carried on by members of his immediate family who are in constant contact with the President,[40] the no-new-foreign-deals pledge has turned out to be an empty promise,[41] and far from being unaware of his holdings and how they are doing, the President regularly visits many of his properties.[42]

39. The Editors, Donald Trump's New York Times Interview: Full Transcript, N.Y. Times (Nov. 23, 2016), https://www.nytimes.com/2016/11/23/us/politics/trump-new-york-times-interview-transcript.html.

40. For a summary as of July 2017, see Kate Brannen, Trump Family's Endless Conflicts of Interest: Chapter and Verse, Newsweek, July 3, 2017, at http://www.newsweek.com/trump-familys-endless-conflicts-interest-chapter-and-verse-631216.

41. See Jeremy Venook, Donald Trump's Conflicts of Interest: A Crib Sheet, The Atlantic, Jun 28, 2017, at https://www.theatlantic.com/business/archive/2017/06/donald-trump-conflicts-of-interests/508382/.

42. Sam Petulla, Tracking President Trump's Visits to Trump Properties, NBC News, Jul 3 2017, at http://www.nbcnews.com/politics/donald-trump/how-much-time-trump-spending-trump-properties-n753366.

Perhaps unsurprisingly, a number of foreign states and officials have switched their business to Trump-owned or -branded properties.

The U.S. Constitution contains two clauses that are designed to prevent financial conflicts of interest and both the appearance and the reality of financial corruption. These are the Foreign and Domestic Emoluments Clauses of Article I, section 9, clause 8, and Article 2, section 1, clause 7.

The Foreign Emoluments Clause, Article I, section 9, clause 8, provides that "no Person holding any Office of Profit or Trust under [the United States], shall, without the Consent of the Congress, accept of any present, Emolument, Office, or Title, of any kind whatever, from any King, Prince, or foreign State."

During the Philadelphia Convention, on August 23, 1787, Charles Pinckney "urged the necessity of preserving foreign Ministers & other officers of the U.S. independent of external influence," and he moved to insert a provision which ultimately became Article I, section 9, clause 8.[43] This language was similar to that in Article VI of the Articles of Confederation, except that the new version applied only to federal officers, and allowed Congress to authorize exceptions.[44] The proposed language was adopted without objection.

At the Virginia ratifying convention, Governor Randolph explained that "[t]his restriction was provided to prevent corruption. . . . An accident, which actually happened, operated in producing the restriction. A box was presented to our ambassador by the king of our allies. It was thought proper, in order to exclude corruption and foreign influence, to prohibit any one in office from receiving or holding any emoluments from foreign states."[45] Randolph was apparently referring to the gift of a very expensive diamond encrusted snuffbox, with a portrait of King Louis XVI, that had been given by the King to then-Ambassador Benjamin Franklin.[46]

The reason for prohibiting all such gifts in advance (at least without congressional "Consent"), Randolph explained, was that one could not rely on individual ministers to turn down such gifts when they were bestowed: "I believe, that if at that moment, when we were in harmony with the King of France, we had supposed that he was corrupting our ambassador, it might have disturbed that confidence, and diminished that mutual friendship, which contributed to carry us through the war."

In his commentaries on the Constitution, St. George Tucker, a Jeffersonian, pointed to the example of Charles II, who was said to be under the pay of Louis XIV: "In the reign of Charles the second of England, that prince, and almost all

---

43. 2 The Records of the Federal Convention of 1787 389 (Max Farrand ed., 1911).

44. Article VI provided: "[N]or shall any person holding any office of profit or trust under the United States, or any of them, accept any present, emolument, office or title of any kind whatever from any King, Prince or foreign State."

45. 2 The Debates of the Several State Conventions on the Adoption of the Federal Constitution 344 (Jonathan Elliot ed., 1937); 3 Farrand 327.

46. Franklin requested and received permission to keep it, even though it is unclear from the text of the Articles of Confederation that Congress could give consent.

his officers of state were either actual pensioners of the court of France, or supposed to be under its influence, directly, or indirectly, from that cause. The reign of that monarch has been, accordingly, proverbially disgraceful to his memory." 1 St. George Tucker, Blackstone's Commentaries 295-96 & n.* (1803; reprint 1996). Tucker explained that "[t]he economy which ought to prevail in republican governments, with respects to salaries and other emoluments of office, might encourage the offer of presents from abroad, if the constitution and laws did not reprobate their acceptance."

The requirement of congressional consent serves two functions. First, it gives federal officials an excuse to turn down or donate gifts without offending foreign governments. Second, requiring Congress to consider the matter draws public attention to attempts to influence federal officials. Publicity gives federal officials incentives to avoid the appearance of impropriety. Moreover, even when Congress permits officials to accept foreign gifts or emoluments, the transparency that comes with congressional deliberation and approval makes it more likely that federal officials will not be influenced by a foreign state's generosity in their official conduct.

As of July 2019, Congress had not passed any resolutions with respect to Trump's holdings or income derived from them.

The Domestic Emoluments Clause of Article 2, section 1, clause 7, states that "The President shall, at stated Times, receive for his Services, a Compensation, which shall neither be increased nor diminished during the Period for which he shall have been elected, and he shall not receive within that Period any other Emolument from the United States, or any of them."

Unlike the Foreign Emoluments Clause, the Domestic Emoluments Clause applies only to the President, and Congress cannot make exceptions by giving its consent. In *The Federalist* 73, Alexander Hamilton explained that the requirement of fixed compensation was designed to prevent corruption of the President either by threats or temptations: Congress and the states "will have no power to alter it, either by increase or diminution, till a new period of service by a new election commences. They can neither weaken his fortitude by operating on his necessities, nor corrupt his integrity by appealing to his avarice. Neither the Union, nor any of its members, will be at liberty to give, nor will he be at liberty to receive, any other emolument than that which may have been determined by the first act."

Several lawsuits have been filed charging President Trump with violations of the Foreign and/or Domestic Emoluments Clause. One suit, *CREW v. Trump*, 276 F.Supp.3d 174 (S.D.N.Y. 2017), was brought by Citizens for Responsibility and Ethics in Washington (CREW), a progressive government-watchdog organization. They have been joined by an association of restaurants and restaurant workers and by a person who books events at various hotels that compete with Trump-branded properties for business from foreign guests and state officials staying in Washington, D.C. They allege that Trump's violations of the Foreign and Domestic Emoluments Clauses harm their economic interests. The district court dismissed the Domestic Emoluments Clause claims for lack of standing, and the Foreign

Emoluments Clause claims because they were both a non-justiciable political question and, in the alternative, not ripe for judicial resolution. As of the summer of 2019, the case was on appeal before the Second Circuit.

A second suit, *District of Columbia v. Trump*, 291 F.Supp.3d 725 (D. Maryland 2018), was brought by the Attorney Generals of the District of Columbia and Maryland, respectively. They argue that the President's Trump International Hotel in Washington, near the White House, draws business from taxpayer-financed convention centers and facilities in D.C. and Maryland. The hotel gives the President income both from foreign countries and officials, and from state and local government officials, who might be eager to please him.

D.C. and Maryland also argue that Trump's business practices generate pressure and competition among state and local governments to provide the Trump Organization with concessions and exemptions in taxation, environmental protection, land use, and zoning. This undermines their budgets, tax revenues, and regulatory authority. They argue that "the Domestic Emoluments Clause aims to prevent 'the United States, or any of them,' from feeling compelled (or being compelled) to confer private financial benefits on the President in order to compete for influence and favor."

In this case, the district court held that plaintiffs had standing to raise claims under the "Foreign and Domestic Emoluments Clauses of the Constitution by reason of [the President's] involvement with and receipt of benefits from the Trump International Hotel and its appurtenances in Washington, D.C. as well as the operations of the Trump Organization with respect to the same." At the same time, it held that "Plaintiffs lack standing to challenge possible constitutional violations by the President involving operations of the Trump Organization outside the District of Columbia from which the President may receive personal benefits." Finally, the court held that the surviving claims were not barred by the political question doctrine. On appeal, the Fourth Circuit dismissed the plaintiffs' claims for lack of standing. See District of Columbia v. Trump, 2019 WL 2998602 (4th Cir. 2019); In re Trump, 2019 WL 2997909 (4th Cir. 2019).

A third suit, *Blumenthal v. Trump*, No. 1:17-cv-01154 (D.D.C. 2017), was brought by the Constitutional Accountability Center (CAC), a liberal public-interest organization devoted to constitutional issues. The plaintiffs in the suit include approximately 160 Congressmen and 30 senators, led by Connecticut Senator Richard Blumenthal and Michigan Congressman John Conyers. All are Democrats. The plaintiffs seek to enforce the Foreign Emoluments Clause. They argue that President Trump is receiving many different kinds of profits for his businesses from foreign governments and officials—many of whom wish to curry favor with him—but that the President has made no effort to seek Congress's permission or to provide Congress with the information necessary to judge whether he is in compliance with the Constitution. Their complaint argues that "[b]ecause Defendant has failed to come to Congress and seek consent before accepting foreign emoluments that have been confirmed through public reporting, it is impossible to know whether Defendant is accepting other foreign emoluments that have not yet been made public. Indeed, through his personal attorney, Defendant has indicated that he does not believe the Constitution requires him to seek or obtain Congress's consent before accepting benefits arising out of exchanges between foreign states and his businesses." The District Court subsequently held that the controversy was justiciable, and that the plaintiffs had standing. Blumenthal v. Trump, 335 F.Supp.3d 45, 72 (D.D.C. 2018).

Discussion

1. *Standing.* All three suits raise important standing questions. Under the Supreme Court's modern doctrine, standing to bring suit under Article III of the Constitution requires that the plaintiff show three things: First, the plaintiff must have suffered an "injury in fact"—an invasion of a legally-protected interest which is (a) concrete and particularized, and (b) actual or imminent, not conjectural or hypothetical. Second, there must be a causal connection between the injury and the conduct complained of; the injury has to be fairly traceable to the challenged action of the defendant, and not the result of the independent action of some third party not before the court. Third, it must be likely, as opposed to merely speculative, that the injury will be redressed by a favorable decision. Lujan v. Defenders of Wildlife, 504 U. S. 555, 560-61 (1992). These three requirements are usually referred to for short as the requirements of (1) injury-in-fact, (2) causation and (3) redressability.

Do the *CREW* and *D.C.* plaintiffs have standing to challenge violations of the Foreign and Domestic Emoluments Clauses?

One might assume that the answer is yes, because the Emoluments Clauses are designed to benefit *all* Americans by ensuring that their elected officials are not unduly influenced by considerations that might conflict with the best interests of the nation as a whole. On this view, we are all injured if those officials are beholden to foreign powers or otherwise diverted from serving the public interest. The Supreme Court, however, has in recent decades repeatedly held that a "generalized grievance" in *seeing that officials obey the law*, suffered in common by all Americans, or by all taxpayers, is insufficient to establish Article III standing for any one of those aggrieved Americans. In such cases, the Court has reasoned, "the political process, rather than the judicial process, may provide the more appropriate remedy for a widely shared grievance."

Accordingly, the plaintiffs in the emoluments litigation would only have standing to challenge those violations that in some way affect them *personally*. So, for example, if the Philippines agrees to make it easier for the Trump Organization to build a new hotel in Manila that might produce lots of income, or Chinese officials decide to play on Trump golf courses in Scotland or New Jersey, it is not immediately apparent how such conduct would harm the plaintiffs personally and distinctly, even if President Trump's receipt of the income does violate the Foreign Emoluments Clause.

It is plausible to think that Trump's hotel in D.C. might hurt local businesses because it draws away business from foreign and state officials eager to ingratiate themselves with the Trump Administration. But is the economic loss caused by Trump's acceptance of the extra profits? If a court required the Trump

Organization to disgorge any profits from foreign and state officials, isn't it possible that at least some of these foreign and state officials would keep patronizing Trump's establishments anyway, just to please him? If so, then plaintiffs may not have shown causation and redressability. What is the plaintiffs' best response? (Hint: Consider changing the kind of remedy that plaintiffs seek.)[47] What do you make of D.C. and Maryland's other argument under the Domestic Emoluments Clause — that they are harmed by having to compete with other jurisdictions in offering tax breaks and regulatory concessions?[48]

Blumenthal v. Trump presents a different set of standing issues. Here the question is whether a group of individual members of Congress — not Congress as a whole or even one House — have standing to enforce the Foreign Emoluments Clause. In Raines v. Byrd, 521 U. S. 811 (1997), the Supreme Court held that six individual Members of Congress lacked standing to challenge the Line Item Veto Act. It "attach[ed] some importance to the fact that [the Raines plaintiffs had] not been authorized to represent their respective Houses of Congress." Id., at 829. "[I]ndeed," the Court observed, "both houses actively oppose[d] their suit." Id. Thus, the plaintiffs were asserting the institutional interests of Congress as a whole even though Congress did not want to assert those interests or did not believe that they were injured. By contrast, in Arizona Legislature v. Arizona Redistricting Commission, 135 S.Ct. 2652 (2015), the Supreme Court distinguished *Raines* and upheld the standing of the *entire* Arizona Legislature to protect its authority under the Elections Clause, Art. I, §4, cl. 1, to establish redistricting maps for federal House seats.[49] The Arizona legislature, the Court explained, "is an institutional plaintiff asserting an institutional injury, and it commenced this action after authorizing votes in both of its chambers." Is *Blumenthal v. Trump* closer to *Raines* or *Arizona Legislature*? Does the currently Republican-controlled Congress want to oversee Trump? If not, then does this mean that that the *Blumenthal* plaintiffs will have to wait until Trump's political opponents control both Houses of Congress? See also Virginia House Of Delegates v. Bethune-Hill, 139 S.Ct. 1945 (2019)(holding that a single house of the Virginia legislature lacked standing to contest a state redistricting plan).

2. *Political Question Doctrine.* The Supreme Court's 1962 decision in Baker v. Carr, 369 U.S. 186, 217 (1962) described six circumstances in which a legal issue might be nonjusticiable because it is a political question: (1) where the Constitution makes a textually demonstrable constitutional commitment of the

47. See Leah Littman, On Standing In CREW v. Trump Part I: Defining The Injury, Take Care, April 27, 2017, https://takecareblog.com/blog/on-standing-in-crew-v-trump-part-i-defining-the-injury.

48. There are additional theories of standing based on Maryland's sovereign and quasi-sovereign interests. For a discussion, see Laurence H. Tribe and Joshua Matz, Maryland and DC Have Standing to Sue Trump for Emoluments Violations, Take Care, June 12, 2017, https://takecareblog.com/blog/maryland-and-dc-have-standing-to-sue-trump-for-emoluments-violations.

49. See Art. I, §4, cl. 1 ("The Times, Places and Manner of holding Elections for Senators and Representatives, shall be prescribed in each State by the Legislature thereof"). The legislature argued that an Amendment to the Arizona Constitution by a statewide popular initiative, which had transferred the redistricting function to an expert commission, violated the Elections Clause.

issue to another branch of government; (2) where there is a lack of judicially dis-coverable and manageable standards for resolving it; (3) where the court would have to make a policy determination of a kind clearly for nonjudicial discretion; (4) where a decision would be disrespectful to coordinate branches of govern-ment; (5) where there is an unusual need to treat a political branch's decision as final; and (6) where it is necessary for the federal government to speak with one voice on an issue. In Zivotofsky v. Clinton, 132 S. Ct. 1421, 1427-28 (*Zivotofsky I*) (2012), the Court maintained that the first two of these six factors are virtually determinative, and emphasized that the political question doctrine is "a narrow exception to [the] rule" that "the Judiciary has a responsibility to decide cases properly before it, even those it 'would gladly avoid.'"

Whether a President has violated the Foreign Emoluments Clause may turn on whether Congress gives its consent. Therefore, one might argue that the Constitution has assigned *to Congress* the exclusive power to decide whether something is an "emolument" and whether the President may accept it. Application of the Clause often implicates delicate foreign relations, which are inappropriate for courts to handle.

On the other hand, Congress's ability to bless what would otherwise be a vio-lation of the Emoluments Clause doesn't mean that Congress is the sole check on Presidential corruption. Moreover, Congress has by statute permitted a range of transactions for various federal officials, and cases construing these statutes are almost certainly justiciable.

In any case, this argument would not affect claims under the Domestic Emoluments Clause, under which congressional consent is immaterial. (Would it make sense if courts could adjudicate Domestic Emoluments Clause cases, but not those involving foreign enticements?)

A second and related argument for treating the clauses as non-justiciable is that, unless Congress specifically passes a statute governing gifts to Presidents, the sole remedy for violations of both clauses is impeachment and removal.

The problem with this theory is that it would give bad incentives to unscru-pulous Presidents.[50] If courts can rule on emoluments claims, presidents would have an incentive to get permission from both houses of Congress before accept-ing gifts from foreign governments. If the President does not wait, he or she will be subject to a lawsuit (assuming, of course, that someone has standing to sue). If the question is not justiciable, however, the incentives would work in the opposite direction. Presidents could accept gifts and dare Congress to impeach and remove (or they could just keep the income and gifts secret). It is politically very hard to impeach a president, and even harder to remove one. To be sure, Congress might try to pass a statute that limits the President's conduct and requires disclosure of income from foreign governments. But because the President can veto any such law, Congress would have to obtain a two-thirds

---

50. Richard Primus, Two thoughts on the Government's Motion to Dismiss in the CREW emolu-ments case, Balkinization, June 9, 2017, https://balkin.blogspot.com/2017/06/two-thoughts-on-gov-ernments-motion-to.html .

majority in both houses—a even larger majority in the House than is required for impeachment. In short, although the Clause contemplates that Presidents will not accept foreign gifts or emoluments unless both houses of Congress give permission, holding that the Clause is nonjusticiable would render this requirement effectively irrelevant.

3. *Does the Foreign Emoluments Clause apply to the President?* The text of the Domestic Emoluments Clause clearly applies to the President. It has long been assumed by Congress and the Executive Branch that the President holds an "Office of Profit or Trust under" the United States and therefore the Foreign Emoluments Clause applies to the President as well. Moreover, this reading is consistent with the central purpose of the Clause—to prevent foreign influence and corruption.

Nevertheless, Seth Barrett Tillman has recently argued that the Clause does not actually apply to the President, because although he is an "Officer," he does not hold an "Office of Profit or Trust under" the United States.[51] Tillman's view is that the latter group includes only appointed officials, not elected officials such as the President, Vice President, and members of Congress. Tillman points out that President George Washington received the key to the French Bastille and a portrait of Louis XVI from French officials without asking Congress's permission—apparently without anyone raising a constitutional objection. It is of course possible that Congress found it imprudent to object to Washington's probity; nevertheless these examples offer an argument from early practice that might gloss the text.

One difficulty with the argument is that it might prove too much.[52] If the President does not hold an "Office of Profit or Trust" under the United States, then the rest of the clause doesn't apply either. This means that foreign governments could hire the President as an employee and give him or her foreign titles of nobility as well. The idea that the President could accept a foreign title from the King of England (for example) would have been unthinkable to the Framers. (Incidentally, the Titles of Nobility Clause, which immediately precedes the Foreign Emoluments Clause in Article I, section 9, clause 8, says only that "No Title of Nobility shall be granted by the *United States*." The ban on accepting foreign titles is in the Emoluments Clause.)

For this reason, the Justice Department has long taken the position that the President is bound by both the Foreign and the Domestic Emoluments Clauses. As a result, when President Barack Obama won the Nobel Prize in 2009 (along with an award of approximately 1.4 million dollars), it raised a Foreign Emoluments Clause question. The OLC issued an opinion explaining that he could keep the

---

51. Seth Barrett Tillman, The Original Public Meaning Of The Foreign Emoluments Clause: A Reply To Professor Zephyr Teachout, 107 Nw. L. Rev. Colloquy 180 (2013).

52. See Marty Lederman, How the DOJ Brief in CREW v. Trump Reveals that Donald Trump is Violating the Foreign Emoluments Clause, Take Care, June 12, 2017, https://takecareblog.com/blog/how-the-doj-brief-in-crew-v-trump-reveals-that-donald-trump-is-violating-the-foreign-emoluments-clause.

prize because the Nobel Committee that awards the Peace Prize was not a "King, Prince, or Foreign State" under the meaning of the Clause. Obama nevertheless donated the proceeds to charity.[53]

4. *What is an Emolument?* The final question is whether President Trump accepts an "emolument" when he benefits from profits flowing to Trump-owned and licensed businesses, or from concessions, benefits, and tax breaks to Trump-owned and licensed businesses.

John Mikhail has argued that the predominant meaning of the term "emolument" at the time of the founding was "anything of value," and that this is how the term was frequently used by Blackstone and by various Framers.[54] Under this definition, if the President receives anything of value from a foreign or state government, this violates the Foreign and Domestic Emoluments Clauses, respectively.[55]

If one accepts this definition, however, it is still necessary to adopt some sort of limiting construction. Otherwise, the clauses would produce any number of implausible results. It would follow, for example, that federal officials could not, without congressional consent, own index or other mutual funds that included any companies that do business globally. A President could not own federal or state bonds because interest from the bonds would violate the Domestic Emoluments Clause. And officials could not receive royalties for books — even from books written and published before they took office — because some foreign or state government's library might have purchased the book. A simple reading of "emolument" as "anything of value" is too broad. Hence, the key substantive issue in *CREW* and other cases is what kind of limiting construction courts should adopt.

The employment theory. A relatively narrow construction would be that "emolument" refers only to compensation for services rendered in an employment or consulting relationship. Hence, the President violates the Foreign Emoluments Clause when he or she receives compensation for services arising

---

53. *See* Applicability of the Emoluments Clause and the Foreign Gifts and Decorations Act to the President's Receipt of the Nobel Peace Prize 33 Op. O.L.C. 1 (2009); Alister Bull and Mohammad Zargham, *Obama gives $1.4 million Nobel prize to 10 charities*, REUTERS, Mar 11th, 2010, http://www.reuters.com/article/us-obama-donation-idUSTRE62A5EN20100311.

54. John Mikhail, A Note on the Original Meaning of "Emolument," Balkinization, January 18, 2017, https://balkin.blogspot.com/2017/01/a-note-on-original-meaning-of-emolument.html; John Mikhail, Other uses of "emolument" in The Federalist (and the fallacy of affirming the consequent), Balkinization, January 25, 2017, https://balkin.blogspot.com/2017/01/other-uses-of-emolument-in-federalist.html ; John Mikhail, "Emolument" in Blackstone's Commentaries, May 28, 2017, https://balkin.blogspot.com/2017/05/emolument-in-blackstones-commentaries.html.

55. See District of Columbia v. Trump,315 F.Supp.3d 875, 900 (D. Maryland 2018)("An 'emolument' within the meaning of the Emoluments Clauses was intended to reach be-yond simple payment for services rendered by a federal official in his official capacity, which in effect would merely restate a prohibition against bribery. The term was in-tended to embrace and ban anything more than de minimis profit, gain, or advantage offered to a public official in his private capacity as well, wholly apart from his official salary."). Accord, Blumenthal v. Trump, 373 F. Supp. 3d 191, 207 (D.D.C. 2019)(" 'Emolument' is broadly defined as any profit, gain, or advantage.").

out of an employment or consulting relationship with a foreign government. See Andy Grewal, The Foreign Emoluments Clause and the Chief Executive, SSRN, January 19, 2017, at https://papers.ssrn.com/sol3/papers.cfm?abstract_id=2902391. These situations, in which the President is directly in the pay of a foreign power, are likely to be very rare.

The nexus theory. In the *CREW* litigation, the Department of Justice has taken the view that an emolument need not require an employment or consulting relationship with a foreign government. It can also cover "benefits arising from services the President provides to [a] foreign state . . . as President (e.g., making executive decisions favorable to the paying foreign power)." "Neither the text nor the history of the Clauses," the DOJ explains, "shows that they were intended to reach benefits arising from a President's private business pursuits having nothing to do with his office or personal service to a foreign power." That is because "the evils sought to be prevented by the Clause are inducements in the forms of pecuniary compensation and other benefits for the President's services *as President*, as such benefits would pose the greatest danger of undermining the President's independence." Therefore, the DOJ argues, there must be a *nexus* between the payments or benefits that flow to the President and his or her office as President. Relying heavily on *one* definition in a handful of Founding-era dictionaries, the DOJ argues that an "emolument" includes any profit *"arising from* an office or employ" or the "receipt of value for services rendered or for a position held."

Under the DOJ's account, the fact that Trump obtains income from foreign officials staying at his hotels is not an emolument; nor is China's decision to authorize trademarks for Trump Organization businesses. The money does not flow to the President in his official capacity or because of any actions he has taken in his official capacity as President.

On the other hand, the CREW plaintiffs allege that foreign governments are shifting their business to Trump properties and that China has granted trademarks *in order to curry favor with the President*—that is, in the hope that he will use his official powers in ways that will benefit them (or not harm them). According to the CREW plaintiffs, then, the profits *do* "arise from" Trump's office, and thus satisfy even the DOJ's definition, because the President receives these benefits as a result of his office, not in spite of it.[56]

To avoid this conclusion, the DOJ argues that plaintiffs must also show that the money flowed to Trump as compensation for *actions* he takes as President. It may be very difficult to prove that the President actually changed his decision-making because of the money flowing to his businesses from foreign governments. If the DOJ's nexus test requires this, it would make the Foreign Emoluments Clause largely unenforceable, absent proof of a deliberate quid pro quo.

The functional theory. A different view of the two clauses would be functional: an emolument is any income, gift or present that might have the potential

---

56. See Lederman, *supra*, note 9.

of influencing or corrupting the integrity of the recipient, whether or not the income arises out of their actions as an officer.[57] This is the view that the Office of Legal Counsel (OLC) took in a 1981 opinion about the Domestic Emoluments Clause.[58] It argued that President Reagan could receive California state retirement benefits arising from his service as governor of California because the income was already vested before he became President, and could not be withdrawn by the state. Therefore, there was no danger that it could influence his decisionmaking.[59]

In 1993, the OLC held that the Foreign Emoluments Clause prevented members of the Administrative Conference (who are government officers operating in a federal agency) from drawing shares of their law firms' profits because those firms had clients who were foreign governments and money from client services went into the partnership pool.[60] The prohibition applied even though the officials "did not personally represent a foreign government, . . . had no personal contact with that client of the firm, [and] could not be said to be subject to the foreign government's 'control' in his or her activities on behalf of the partnership." Rather, the OLC argued, "[m]ore important . . . is the fact that the Conference member would draw a proportionate share of the partnership's pooled profits, which would include any profits the firm earned from representing its foreign governmental client. Because the amount the Conference member would receive from the partnership's profits would be a function of the amount paid to the firm by the foreign government, the partnership would in effect be a conduit for that government. Thus, some portion of the member's income could fairly be attributed to a foreign government." Presumably, the practical concern was that if a foreign government were unhappy with the Conference's work, it could switch law firms, affecting the partnership pool, and creating indirect pressure on the official from the partnership.

Which of these accounts best serves the purposes of the two Clauses? Which is likely to produce the most coherent and administrable doctrine?

57. See Jane Chong, Reading the Office of Legal Counsel on Emoluments: Do Super-Rich Presidents Get a Pass?, Lawfare, July 1, 2017, https://lawfareblog.com/reading-office-legal-counsel-emoluments-do-super-rich-presidents-get-pass.

58. President Reagan's Ability to Receive Retirement Benefits from the State of California, 5 Op. O.L.C. 187 (1981).

59. See District of Columbia v. Trump, 315 F. Supp. at 904 ("Based on precedent from the OLC and Comptroller General, there would be an exception, at least under the Domestic Emoluments Clause, where the thing of value received by the federal office holder, after the fashion of the Reagan-California pension precedent, was fully vested and indefeasi-ble before the federal official became a federal official, the rationale being that the ben-efit would lack any potential to influence the federal office-holder in his decision-making.")

60. Applicability of the Emoluments Clause to Non-Government Members of ACUS, 17 Op. O.L.C. 114, 119 (1993).

Replace Note on Presidential Impeachment on p. 1015 with the following:

Note: Presidential Impeachment

Article II, section 4 states that "The President, Vice President and all civil officers of the United States, shall be removed from Office on Impeachment for, and Conviction of, Treason, Bribery, or other high Crimes and Misdemeanors." Article I prescribes that the House of Representatives is entrusted with the power to impeach, the Senate with the power to try impeachments, and the Chief Justice of the Supreme Court acts as the presiding officer at Presidential impeachments.

Two presidents, Andrew Johnson and Bill Clinton, have been impeached by the House. No President has ever been convicted and removed by the Senate. Richard Nixon resigned to avoid impeachment.

This Note discusses the history of the two most recent impeachment controversies, the structural issues involved in impeachment, and finally, the meaning of "high Crimes and Misdemeanors" as the potential grounds for impeachment.[61]

1. Two modern impeachments. The two modern impeachment controversies involved Richard Nixon and Bill Clinton.

a. Nixon's resignation. The House Judiciary Committee voted to recommend the first of three articles of impeachment of President Richard Nixon to the full House on July 27, 1974. The primary accusation was that Nixon had attempted to cover up and impede the investigation of the burglary at the Watergate Hotel in July 1972, when five men broke into the Democratic National Committee headquarters at the Watergate office complex in Washington. Nixon attempted to cover up his Administration's involvement in the burglary.

The Watergate scandal ultimately led to the discovery of multiple abuses of power by the Nixon Administration, including secret wiretapping of political activists, and the use of the FBI, the CIA, and the IRS to investigate and/or harass political opponents. Ultimately, 69 people were indicted, leading to 48 convictions, including Attorney General John Mitchell, the President's chief of staff, H.R. Haldeman, the President's chief domestic policy advisor, John Ehrlichman, and many other high Administration officials.

Upon the revelation that Nixon had taped many of his conversations in the Oval Office, a protracted legal and political struggle began to get access to the Watergate tapes. Nixon resisted until the Supreme Court ordered him to hand over the tapes in United States v Nixon on July 24, 1974. The White House finally complied on August 5, 1974. The tapes revealed, among other things, that

---

61. For two recent studies of the law of impeachment, see Cass R. Sunstein, Impeachment: A Citizen's Guide (2017); Laurence Tribe and Joshua Matz, To End a Presidency: The Power of Impeachment (2018). A classic account from 1974 is Charles L. Black, Jr. Impeachment: A Handbook, Philip Bobbitt, ed. (2d ed. 2018). See also the discussion of the Clinton impeachment in Akhil Reed Amar, The Constitution Today: Timeless Lessons for the Issues of Our Era 273-326 (2016).

Nixon had ordered the CIA to get the FBI to stop investigating the Watergate burglary on grounds of national security; and that Nixon had ordered his aides to engage in a cover up. At this point Nixon's faced almost certain impeachment in the House and conviction in the Senate. Political leaders in his own party now urged him to give up the fight. He resigned on August 8, 1974. This avoided impeachment by the full House. His former Vice-President, President Gerard Ford, pardoned him a month later, on September 8, 1974. As a result, Nixon never faced criminal prosecution.

   b. Clinton's impeachment and acquittal. In the most recent presidential impeachment in 1998, the House impeached Bill Clinton for perjury and obstruction of justice arising out of his affair with a White House intern, Monica Lewinsky. In a deposition arising out of a sexual harassment lawsuit brought by Paula Jones, Clinton had denied having "sexual relations" with Lewinsky. That lawsuit was later settled out of court. However, Independent Counsel Kenneth Starr, who had been investigating the Whitewater land deal, learned that Clinton and Lewinsky had an affair. He convened a grand jury, threatened Lewinsky with prosecution for false testimony in the Jones lawsuit, and reached an immunity deal in return for her grand jury testimony. Lewinsky testified that she had engaged in various forms of intimate physical relations with the President. Before the grand jury, Clinton testified that his statements during the Jones deposition were technically accurate (because of the convoluted definition of "sexual relations" and related terms that the attorneys had agreed to in that case). However, he admitted to "inappropriate contact" with Lewinsky. Starr issued a report to Congress on September 9, 1998, detailing his findings and grounds for impeachment of Clinton.

   The House began impeachment hearings on October 8, 1998, which were marked by acrimony between Democrats and Republicans. In the November 1998 mid-term elections, the Republicans lost five seats in the House. Opposition parties in the sixth term of a presidency usually gain twenty or more seats, so this was regarded as an unusually poor showing. Many commentators blamed the rebuff on the national party's decision to make Clinton and the Lewinsky affair an issue in selected House races; and public opinion polls suggested that the public was wearying of months of media coverage of the scandal and that a substantial majority opposed impeachment.

   Apparently, although the public had a low opinion of Clinton's ethics, his approval ratings as President remained high. Nevertheless, the House hearings continued after the election under the leadership of the lame duck Congress, and in December 1998, a bitterly divided Congress passed two of four proposed articles of impeachment, essentially along party lines, with almost all Republicans supporting impeachment and almost all Democrats opposing it. The two articles accused Clinton of perjuring himself before the grand jury and of obstructing justice. On February 12, 1999, the Senate voted to acquit Clinton of both charges. The vote was 55 for acquittal and 45 for conviction on the perjury count, and 50-50 on the obstruction of justice count. Once again the votes were strongly partisan: all 45 Democrats voted for acquittal on both counts and most Republicans voted for conviction.

2. *The House's Role.* How should responsible members of the House of Representatives think about their vote?

Here it is important to distinguish between impeachments of presidents and impeachments of judges. In fact, there have been many more impeachments of judges than of presidents—some fifteen in all—and many more judges have been investigated without impeachment.[62]

One might think that judicial independence requires that judges should not be removed for political reasons. (This is one of the lessons of the Chase impeachment in the early Republic, see Casebook, p. 116). By contrast, the impeachment of a president sits between a legal and a political judgment and has aspects of both. Moreover, although impeachment is akin to a judicial proceeding, it is not part of the Article III process for judging disputes. It takes place in an Article I institution—part of the representative and political branches.

Under Article I, the House can impeach the President by a simple majority. Note that conviction by the Senate requires a two-thirds vote. Does this suggest that the standard of proof for the House is different than for the Senate?

If one adopts a judicial model, one might argue that the House is equivalent to a grand jury considering an indictment. Under this analogy, it needs only probable cause to believe that the President (or other officer) has committed an impeachable offense. On the other hand, there are significant differences between the House and a grand jury. There is no prosecutor to guide the House; thus House members must play both the role of prosecutor and grand jury. (Query: Why couldn't an Independent Counsel like Kenneth Starr play that role? Think about the separation of powers discussions following Morrison and Edmond in Chapter Six, pp. 892-98, 901).

Because the House must play two roles, its considerations are arguably different from those of a grand jury. Moreover, the House is an elected body whose members take an oath to uphold the Constitution and also owe responsibilities to their constituents. See Neil S. Siegel, After the Trump Era: A Constitutional Role Morality for Presidents and Members of Congress, 107 Geo. L. J. 109 (2018). Are there tensions in these duties?

There is also the question of hijacking the nation's attention and agenda. Here again, we should distinguish between impeaching judges and impeaching presidents. A president has been elected by the people and removal from office through impeachment short-circuits the democratic process, and so may be deeply divisive. The House must decide whether it is worth it to put the country through a presidential impeachment. Obviously, impeachments of both presidents and

---

62. See Impeachments of Federal Judges, Federal Judicial Center, https://www.fjc.gov/history/judges/impeachments-federal-judges (listing impeachments); Warren S. Grimes, Hundred-Ton-Gun Control: Preserving Impeachment as the Exclusive Removal Mechanism for Federal Judges, 38 U.C.L.A. L. Rev. 1209, 1216 (1991)(compiling numbers of federal judges investigated for impeachment up to 1989).

judges cost the Senate valuable time, but presidential impeachments in particular are likely to consume the lion's share of the Senate's time and attention.

Should a conscientious House member vote against impeachment if he or she believes that the Senate will not convict? Or should the member vote for impeachment on the grounds that there is an independent constitutional duty to say what the appropriate legal standard is?

Consider the possibility that House members in Clinton's case might have voted for impeachment on the ground that (1) they knew the Senate would not convict, or (2) that they wanted to show their disapproval of Clinton akin to a motion for censure. Is either or both of these reasons constitutionally appropriate?

Is it appropriate for the House to begin impeachment proceedings to get access to information from the President when the President refuses to cooperate with oversight investigations? In *U.S. v. Nixon*, the Court held that executive privilege must yield to the need for information in an ongoing criminal investigation. Does the same logic apply to an impeachment investigation, which, as noted above, is akin to a judicial proceeding?

3. Impeachment as a Political Act. To what extent should impeachment and conviction depend on the President's popularity? On the public's view whether the President should not be impeached and/or convicted? Compare Charles L. Black, Jr., Impeachment: A Handbook 20 (1974)("taking, at intervals, of public opinion polls on guilt or innocence, should be looked on as an unspeakable indecency.") with Michael J. Klarman, Constitutional Fetishism and the Clinton Impeachment Debate, 85 Va. L. Rev. 631 (1999) ("If popular majorities get to elect a President, it is hard to see why they should be ignored on the question of whether he remains fit to hold office.")

During the impeachment proceedings, President Clinton's approval ratings were quite high, particularly for a President in his sixth year in office. They got even higher as a response to the House's impeachment resolutions. By contrast, President Nixon was deeply unpopular by the time he resigned in August 1974, and politicians of both parties were calling for his resignation.

Consider the following arguments and counterarguments:

(a) *Constitutional obligations.* Impeachment and conviction are constitutional obligations of the House and the Senate, respectively. They cannot be shirked no matter how popular a president is or what his poll numbers might be. A House member must vote for impeachment if there are reasonable grounds for impeachment, and a Senator must convict if he or she believes that the President has committed a high crime or misdemeanor judged by the appropriate standard of proof.

(b) *Prosecutorial Discretion and Jury Deliberation.* Impeachment is a prosecutorial act. Prosecutors engage in prosecutorial discretion all the time, and they should do so in the interests of the public. (See the discussion of the *Cox* and *Nixon* cases in Chapter Six for a list of justifications for prosecutorial discretion). Hence the House must consider whether proceeding with impeachment is for the good of the country. One important consideration is whether House members are going against the will of the people who elected the President to office.

Textually, note that Article I, Section 3 gives the House "the sole Power of Impeachment" but says nothing about any duty to impeach. Intratextually, note that the Framers knew how to use the word "duty"—indeed they used it twice in Article II. On this view, House impeachment is about power, not duty—about choices, not obligations. A related point: The House's inherent power of mercy is all the more vital given that the ordinary locus of pretrial mercy in our constitutional system—the President's pardon power—is inapplicable. As we have seen, under Article II, Section 2, a president may ordinarily pardon at any time and for any reason (recall Gerald Ford's pretrial pardon of Nixon and George Bush's pretrial pardon of Caspar Weinberger), but not "in cases of impeachment." Thus, in impeachment prosecutions, the Framers took the power of executive clemency away from the President and gave it to the House.

Similarly, Senators must consider whether conviction and removal would be in the best interests of the country. If House members are roughly in the role of prosecutors, Senators are roughly in the role of jurors. Like any ordinary criminal juror, each Senator is free to be merciful for a wide variety of reasons—because she thinks the defendant has suffered enough, or because the punishment doesn't fit the crime, or because punishing the defendant would impose unacceptable costs on innocent third parties. Moreover unlike ordinary jurors, Senators are elected, and thus they are also free to consult their constituents. Sometimes, deferring to "the masses" might be irresponsible—for example, if the citizenry were ignorant of the facts or incapable of thinking through the complicated legal question at hand. But Senators should not ignore their constituents where these circumstances do not apply.

(c) *The "Coup' D'Etat" Argument.* Because presidential impeachment is a fundamentally political decision to remove an elected president from office, it should not be undertaken without solid popular support. Although solid popular support may not be sufficient to justify impeachment, it is necessary because impeachment overturns the results of a national election; at the very least it involves a transfer of the most important office in the country without direct popular approval.[63]

Consider the following response: Because of the twelfth and twenty-fifth amendments, the successor to the President will most likely be a member of his own party. (Note that if the President and Vice President are both impeached, the presidency would fall to the Speaker of the House. But see the discussion of presidential succession in Chapter Six).

Compare the impeachments of Bill Clinton and Andrew Johnson. In Clinton's case, Al Gore would have become president. In Johnson's case, there was no vice-president, because the twenty-fifty amendment had not yet been ratified. Johnson was a War Democrat who disagreed with Republicans on many issues. His successor would have been Ben Wade, the Speaker of the House and a Radical Republican who would, most likely, have let the Congress accelerate

63. Jack M. Balkin, "An Implosion of Democracy," Boston Globe, January 17, 1999, at C07.

the process of Reconstruction. (Would Wade's ascension to the Presidency have been a good thing or a bad thing from the standpoint of American democracy?) Note that Andrew Johnson himself had never been elected President by the American people.

Even if a Vice President of the same party succeeds the President, one can still argue that impeachment is a counter-majoritarian assertion that should not proceed without broad popular support. The opposition party may have good reasons to prefer the Vice-President in office, even if he is thereby strengthened for a subsequent run at the presidency. A successful conviction may weaken the presidency and confirm the power of the opposition party. (Consider whether successful conviction of Andrew Johnson in 1868 or Bill Clinton in 1999 would have confirmed the dominance of the Republican Party in either era. Note also that in 1868, putting Ben Wade in White House would have created an obstacle to the election of the Republicans' favored candidate in the 1868 elections, Ulysses S. Grant.)

(d) *The Asymmetrical Importance of Popular Will.* Consider the argument that popular will is most important in cases where it speaks against impeachment and removal of a President:

> If in her heart a Congressperson or Senator thinks the President is innocent in fact (he actually didn't do it) or in law (even if he did it, it is not a "high crime or misdemeanor"), then she must vote not guilty—even if she thereby offends her constituents, who want the man's head. She has taken a solemn oath to do justice, and she would violate that oath if she voted to convict a man she believed innocent. [Moreover, in the Senate] impeachment rules are not symmetric between conviction and acquittal. It takes 67 votes to convict, but only 34 to acquit. On this view, although no Senator may vote to convict a man she deems innocent, any Senator may vote to acquit a man she deems guilty.[64]

(e) *The Political context in which impeachment occurs.* Consider the fact that the Johnson impeachment occurred in the wake of the Civil War, the Nixon resignation during the height of the Cold War, and the Clinton impeachment after the Cold War. Note also the "dog that didn't bark"—the Iran Contra scandal of 1986-87, which did not lead to impeachment proceedings against Ronald Reagan, and which also occurred during the Cold War. To what extent do foreign policy and global military obligations of the United States affect the willingness of Congress to proceed against a sitting President? The Johnson impeachment seems to have been largely about the Republican Congress's desire to have its way on Reconstruction against a President bent on undermining that Reconstruction. (See the discussion of the procedural history of the Fourteenth Amendment in Chapter Four, supra). Is the failure of the Iran-Contra scandal to result in impeachment in part explained on the grounds that Democrats lacked the political will to attack a popular president during the height of the Cold War

---

64. Akhil Reed Amar, The People's Court, Legal Times, Feb. 1, 1999.

unless there was clear proof of the very gravest offenses? If so, what explains the proceedings against Nixon, which also occurred during the Cold War?

One obvious answer is that the offenses in Nixon's case were simply more serious than either Reagan's or Clinton's. However, consider the possibility that Nixon and Clinton had something in common that differentiated them from Reagan. Unlike Reagan, both Nixon and Clinton portrayed themselves as moderates who actively co-opted many of the opposition party's ideas, which infuriated members of the opposition. With the political center effectively occupied by their (despised) ideological opponent, the opposition party turned to scandal as the most effective means of combatting the President. Cf. Stephen Skowronek, The Politics Presidents Make: Leadership from John Adams to George Bush (1993) (explaining that presidents in these circumstances are especially vulnerable to scandal). The danger of such a strategy, however, is that impeachment can make the opposition party look even more partisan. Without capitulation by members of the President's own party, the attack will not succeed and may even backfire.

4. The Senate Trial. Article I, section 3 states that "The Senate shall have the sole Power to try all Impeachments." Does the power to try include a duty to try? Suppose that the President's party has a majority in the Senate and the Senate leadership concludes that there is no chance that the President will be convicted. If the House impeaches, must the Senate hold a trial at all? Can the Senate hold a perfunctory trial leading to a quick vote of acquittal without hearing evidence?

When a president is not being tried, the Constitution specifies in Article I, section 3 that the presiding officer is the Vice President of the United States (who also serves as the president of the Senate.) In presidential impeachments, however, the Chief Justice of the United States, who plays no role in any other impeachment, must "preside" over the Senate trial. There are good structural reasons for this: the Framers excluded the Vice-President from a trial that could end with his winning the defendant's job. This mandatory recusal rule made even more sense at the Founding, when presidents did not handpick their vice presidents, who were more likely to be rivals than partners.

The Constitution specifies that the Chief Justice "shall" preside. Can the Chief Justice refuse, if he or she thinks that the trial is unfair and improper? Could the trial properly proceed without the presence of its constitutionally-prescribed presiding officer? Note that another reason for the chief's presence is also structural: It reminds the Senators that this inherently political trial must be scrupulously fair to the President in both reality and appearance. Not only the American people, but other countries around the world will be watching this test of American democracy.

The role of the Chief Justice has profound implications for the proper ethical relations between senators and the President. Suppose a sudden illness were to require the chief to resign. Although the senior associate justice might presumably fill in temporarily,[65] at some point a new chief would need to be installed. According to Article II, section 2, the President would appoint, with the advice and consent of the Senate, a new chief. In other words, even in the middle of a trial, the judges and the judged might need to confer and collaborate to pick the permanent presiding officer!

This points up a unique feature of Presidential impeachments: the need for coordination between the two branches even as they are at loggerheads. The Senate and the President must work together to do the people's business. Vacant appointments must be filled, treaties considered, laws enacted, budgets approved, foreign policy—even war—conducted. (Note that as the House was considering impeachment of the President, President Clinton was launching airstrikes against terrorist camps halfway around the globe.) Even as senators sit as detached judges and jurors over a presidential defendant every afternoon (bound by an oath of impartiality as prescribed under Article I, section 3), they must as legislators work closely with the President every morning. This also suggests an important difference from impeachments of federal district judges. In these low-level impeachments, senators are more likely to shun all contact with the defendant, analogizing such meetings to "jury tampering."

5. Indictment and Conviction before Impeachment. Presidential and non-presidential impeachments also tend to differ because the latter class of officials can be and often are indicted and convicted before impeachments begin.[66] Presidential impeachments are different. First of all, as discussed below, it is doubtful that an indictable offense is required for impeachment and conviction of the President. Given his unique and awesome constitutional powers, the President can often inflict great harm on the nation without violating any specific criminal statute. As a result, presidential impeachments are less likely to simply track ordinary prosecutions and may more often charge the chief executive with abuses of power beyond the criminal code.

Second, many commentators (and the Justice Department) hold that a sitting president may not be forced to stand trial in an ordinary criminal court. (See also

65. What, precisely, is the basis for this presumption? Pure pragmatism? A structural inference of sorts? The traditions of the Supreme Court, or the history of predecessor courts in England?

66. Indeed, in two of the three district judge impeachments during the 1980s, Senate trials occurred after the judges had been tried and convicted of statutory crimes in ordinary courts. Although the Constitution does not require this sequence, the Framers expected that it would often make sense for geographic reasons. District judges in the late eighteenth century would be scattered across the continent, as would the evidence of and witnesses to their wrongdoing. Congress, by contrast, would sit in the capital, weeks away from the most remote hinterlands. Given this geography, the Founders anticipated that the easiest venue to gather all the evidence and witnesses would often be in a trial held in the judge's home district. See Maria Simon, Note, Bribery and Other Not So "Good Behavior": Criminal Prosecution as a Supplement to Impeachment of Federal Judges, 94 Colum. L. Rev.1617 (1999). After such a trial, the Senate's job in impeachment would be much easier—senators could simply take as given the facts duly found beyond reasonable doubt in an ordinary court following strict evidentiary rules and affording procedural rights and other safeguards to the defendant.

the discussion following Clinton v. Jones, Chapter Six, pp. 1009-1012). In two Federalist Papers (Numbers 69 and 77), Hamilton suggested that an incumbent president must first be tried in the Senate; only after his removal (via conviction or resignation or the natural expiration of his term) would ordinary courts have a opportunity to prosecute him.[67] As noted in the discussion of Clinton v. Jones, there is a structural argument for the rule: A president represents the nation and may need to pursue sound national policies that will render him unpopular in certain localities—consider Lincoln's popularity in South Carolina in early 1861. While in office, the President should not be obstructed by a grand or petit jury from any one locality, whether Charleston or Little Rock or the District of Columbia. The House and the Senate represent the entire nation, and therefore are the only grand and petit juries that a sitting president must answer to.

67. See The Federalist No. 69 ("The President . . .would be liable to be impeached, tried, and upon conviction . . .would afterwards be liable to prosecution and punishment in the ordinary course of law.") (emphasis added); Id. No. 77 (discussing presidential impeachment and "subsequent prosecution in the common course of law") (emphasis added). Note that Hamilton here was trying to reassure his readers that the President would not be overly powerful; if he in fact believed that a sitting President could be forced to stand trial in an ordinary criminal prosecution, he had a strong incentive to say so, but in fact he said the opposite. This impeachment-first rule has a strong bipartisan pedigree—affirmed two centuries ago by Senator (and later Chief Justice) Oliver Ellsworth, Vice President John Adams, and President Thomas Jefferson. See The Diary of William Maclay and Other Notes on Senate Debates 168 (Kenneth R. Bowling & Helen E. Veit eds., 1988) (reporting that Adams and Ellsworth argued that a sitting President could be impeached, but "no other process [w]hatever lay against him. . . .When he is no longer President, [y]ou can indict him."); 10 Works of Thomas Jefferson 404 (Paul L. Ford ed., 1905) (Letter to George Hay, June 20, 1807) ("The leading principle of our Constitution is the independence of the Legislature, executive, and judiciary of each other, and none are more jealous of this than the judiciary. But would the executive be independent of the judiciary, if he were subject to the commands of the latter, [and] to imprisonment for disobedience; if the several courts could bandy him from pillar to post, keep him constantly trudging from north to south [and] east to west.").

The point was reiterated during the Nixon impeachment crisis by then-Solicitor General Robert Bork on the right and Professor Charles Black on the left. See John Hart Ely, On Constitutional Ground 140-41 (1996) (detailing Robert Bork's argument that the President could not be indicted prior to being impeached.); Charles L. Black, Jr., Impeachment: A Handbook 40 (1974)("[A]n incumbent president cannot be put on trial in the ordinary courts for ordinary crime, and if the crime he is charged with is not an impeachable offense, the simple and obvious solution would either be to indict him and delay trial until after his term has expired, or to delay indictment until after his term, with the statute of limitations tolled . . . until the president's term is over."). See also Alexander M. Bickel, the Constitutional Tangle, New Republic, Oct. 6, 1973 (the "presidency cannot be conducted from jail, nor can it be effectively carried on while an incumbent is defending himself in a criminal trial"); Terry Eastland, The Power to Control Prosecution, 2 Nexus 43, 49 (1997) ("the President may be prosecuted, but . . . only to the extent he allows himself to be"); Stephen G. Calabresi, Caesarism, Departmentalism, and Professor Paulsen, 83 Minn. L. Rev. 1421 (1999) ("the President cannot be prosecuted until he has first been impeached and removed"). But see Ronald D. Rotunda, Can a President Plumbing the Constitutional Depths of Clinton v. Jones be Imprisoned?, Legal Times, July 21, 1997 ("Clinton v. Jones thus establishes that a sitting president may be [criminally] indicted and tried"). Compare the discussion in Chapter Six, supra, pointing out some ways in which Jones seems distinguishable.

However, if the President is not subject to trial before impeachment, a Senate trial will (and did in Clinton's case) pose enormous complications concerning issues of evidentiary procedure and proof. The Senate will not be able to simply point to an earlier judicial proceeding that clearly established the relevant facts beyond reasonable doubt. Instead, the Senate is obliged to find the facts for itself. In Clinton's trial, the Senate elected not to hear live witnesses, but instead relied on the record compiled by the House (which drew heavily on the Independent Counsel's report) and videotapes and transcripts of depositions of three witnesses conducted by the House Managers in charge of the President's prosecution.

The Senate is not (unless it chooses to be) bound by federal rules of evidence, including the hearsay rules, which express (with many exceptions) a preference for live testimony subject to cross-examination. Why do you think the Senate did not choose to call witnesses in Clinton's case (and in particular live testimony of Monica Lewinsky, which would, presumably, involve discussions of her affair with President Clinton on national television)? Does this confirm the inherently political nature of presidential impeachments?

By contrast, in the 1980's impeachments of judges the Senate delegated fact-gathering to a committee. Could the Senate do so constitutionally in the case of presidential impeachments? Would it be politically possible to do so even if it were constitutional? Consider whether the committee could meet outside of the presence of the Chief Justice, or whether, on the other hand, the Chief Justice could preside over such a "rump" Senate?

Acting as the jury in an impeachment trial, the Senate also exercises discretion. Even if it considers the President's crimes technically impeachable, it need not vote to convict unless it also thinks that the punishment — mandatory removal from office, under Article II, section 4 — fits the crime. (Analogously, every criminal trial jury has the inherent power to acquit against the evidence if it deems punishment unjust.).

6. *Remedies upon Conviction by the Senate.* As you read Article II, can the Senate convict the President without removing him from office? Can the Senate pass a censure motion in lieu of conviction? Some Senators and Congressmen argued that because the Constitution says nothing about censure, a censure motion was unconstitutional. Why doesn't the fact that the Constitution says nothing about censure mean that nothing prohibits censure? (Note that Andrew Jackson was censured in 1834 by a Whig-controlled Senate for his opposition to the Second Bank, but when the Democrats came to power they removed the censure.).

7. *What are "High Crimes and Misdemeanors"?* The Constitution's language raises two complementary questions. First, are all violations of the criminal code committed by a President High Crimes and Misdemeanors under the meaning of Article II, section 4? One of the central questions in the Clinton impeachment trial was whether perjury about his sexual affair with Monica Lewinsky was a "high Crime and Misdemeanor" under the meaning of Article II, section 4. One

argument that it was not was that the President's perjury, although a crime, was not related to his official duties.[68]

Second, and conversely, must the President's conduct be a crime in order to be a High Crime and Misdemeanor under the meaning of the Constitution? In the Clinton impeachment, for example, the question would have been whether Clinton's behavior—concealing the affair, lying about it to the American people for months, and engaging in evasive maneuvers before Congress and a grand jury constituted impeachable offenses even if they do not technically constitute criminal offenses. In this context, compare President's Trump's evasive behavior and false and misleading statements both before and after he took office, as detailed in the discussion of the Mueller Report, infra.

There are several ways of approaching these questions, corresponding to familiar modalities of constitutional argument.

a. Historical Arguments. The original understandings of the impeachment power are provocative but inconclusive. Several proposals at the Constitutional Convention attempted to limit the grounds for impeachment to neglect of duty or abuse of official power. One proposal argued for limiting the power to "treason or bribery." George Mason opposed this formula and proposed adding "maladministration" to the grounds for impeachment and removal. Madison in turn opposed Mason's amendment, arguing that "[so] vague a term will be equivalent to a tenure during the pleasure of the Senate."

Mason then withdrew his motion and moved to substitute the words "treason, bribery and other high crimes or misdemeanors against the State," which was accepted by the convention. This wording was later changed to "against the United States." Finally, the Committee of Style and Arrangement eliminated the words "against the United States" apparently on the grounds that these words were redundant.

What relevance, if any, should this history have in interpreting Article II, section 4?

Consider the following arguments:

(a) Impeachable offenses must be offenses against the State similar to treason and bribery. Perjury, especially about matters unrelated to the President's duties is much less damaging to the State and hence is not impeachable. What about obstruction of justice?

(b) Impeachable offenses must be offenses against the State, and not merely crimes. Bribery is impeachable only because the President might trade secrets with the enemy or compromise the national interest for private gain. Crimes that are unrelated to the President's duties are not a crimes against the State and is therefore not impeachable.

How do we tell what is unrelated to the President's duties? Suppose the President commits a crime in order to be elected? For example, suppose that

---

68. A separate question is whether one should distinguish between perjury before a deposition in a civil matter and perjury before a grand jury convened by the Independent Counsel.

the President arranges for hush money payments to a former mistress to prevent embarrassing information coming out before the election, and the secret payments violate campaign finance law?

What if the President obstructs investigations into his or his employees' misconduct? Suppose that the President asks his associates to lie before Congress about whether the President was pursuing a real estate deal in Moscow during the presidential campaign? If a cover-up might allow a foreign power leverage over the President, should this be impeachable?

(c) The President is the chief law enforcement officer of the United States and therefore either perjury in official proceedings or obstruction of justice are offenses against the State because they fundamentally undermine confidence in his office and in the government of the United States. (If a President commits any crime to further his political objectives, to hinder his political enemies, or to avoid political embarrassment, should it be regarded as a high crime or misdemeanor?)

(d) Given the language of Article II, section 4, impeachable offenses need not be crimes, much less crimes against the State. A President who abuses his power, or who fundamentally disgraces his office—for example, by raping a person—can be impeached and removed. The question whether the matter is a "public" abuse of power or part of his "private" life is irrelevant.

(e) The question of what a "high Crime and Misdemeanor" consists in is fundamentally political. It is up to the American people, through their elected representatives, to determine when a President has so lost the confidence of the People that he can no longer remain in office.

b. Textual Arguments. The argument that not every crime is impeachable would seem to be bolstered by the following textual argument: Ordinary citizens can be tried and convicted for any crime, but the President may be impeached and removed only for "high" crime. This word must have limiting significance: In two other places in the Constitution (Article I, Section 6 and Article IV, Section 2), the Framers speak about treason and other crimes without using the word "high." This suggests that the adjective was added to the impeachment clause of Article II, Section 4 to make clear that not all crime is impeachable. This argument, however, does not mean that only crimes are impeachable: The word "misdemeanor" is easily read to mean misbehavior or misconduct generally, though it, too, must be "high" misconduct to warrant impeachment.

c. Precedental Arguments. Another approach to the question is to look for precedents in past practice. As noted earlier, in 1998, Bill Clinton was impeached on two counts: perjury and obstruction of justice.

In 1974, the House impeached Richard Nixon on three counts. The first count was obstruction of justice in the covering up and impeding the investigation of the Watergate burglary. The second count was abuse of power: that Nixon had "repeatedly engaged in conduct violating the constitutional rights of citizens, impairing the due and proper administration of justice and the conduct of lawful inquiries, or contravening the laws governing agencies of the executive branch and the purposes of these agencies." The third count was contempt of Congress, stating that Nixon "failed without lawful cause or excuse to produce papers and things as directed by duly authorized subpoenas issued by the Committee on the Judiciary of the House of Representatives on April 11, 1974, May 15, 1974, May 30, 1974, and June 24, 1974, and willfully disobeyed such subpoenas."

d. Precedental and Structural Arguments: Comparing presidents to other kinds of officers. Because there are so few precedents of presidential impeachments, one might look to precedents concerning the impeachments of other officers, including federal judges. However, because these offices have different functions, the precedents may not apply to presidential impeachments. As a result, precedental arguments about the meaning of "high Crimes and Misdemeanors" cannot be easily extricated from structural arguments. (And, as we shall see, each also relies on a series of textual arguments). Hence we consider them together.

Here is an example: During the impeachment proceedings against Richard Nixon, the House Impeachment Committee considered and rejected an article that accused Nixon of backdating his tax returns in order to take advantage of more favorable tax laws. That might suggest that perjury for private gain is not an impeachable offense. On the other hand, during the 1980's two federal judges, Walter Nixon (no relation to Richard) and Alcee Hastings, were impeached and removed for perjury.

One can make a textual argument that high crimes and misdemeanors for presidents and judges should be the same: Article II, section 4 states that "[t]he President, Vice President and all civil officers of the United States, shall be removed from Office on Impeachment for, and Conviction of, Treason, Bribery, or other high Crimes and Misdemeanors." Because Article II, section 4 lumps together presidential impeachments with all others (vice presidents, judges, justices, Cabinet officers, inferior officers) and uses the same linguistic standard (high crimes), the test is the same.

But one can argue in the opposite direction, too: According to Article II, section 2, "by and with the Advice and Consent of the Senate, [the President] shall appoint Ambassadors, other public Ministers and Consuls, Judges of the Supreme Court, and . . . other Officers of the United States." Senators usually give Presidents much more leeway in executive and ambassadorial appointments than judicial appointments, even though the text of the appointments clause is the same for both. If the Senate's Advise and Consent power is different depending on the nature of the office, why not the meaning of High Crimes and Misdemeanors?[69]

---

69. Consider Laurence Tribe's response to this textual argument:

> [A]lthough the Appointments Clause calls in the same words for the Senate's advice and consent regardless of the office involved, that clause says nothing about what standard the Senate is to employ in giving or withholding its consent in any particular category of appointments, and might best be read as agnostic on the question whether that standard is the dependent on the office to which an appointment has been made or is instead to be office-independent. The Impeachment Clause, in contrast, purports to specify the standard for impeachment and removal and seemingly does so in the same terms—"high Crimes and Misdemeanors"—for judges and presidents alike.

1 Laurence H. Tribe, American Constitutional Law 165-69 & n.57 (3rd ed. 1999).

Akhil Amar argues that, quite apart from text, there are good structural grounds for treating presidents and judges differently: "When senators remove one of 1,000 federal judges (or even one of nine justices), they are not transforming an entire branch of government. . . . Presidential impeachments involve high statecraft and international affairs—the entire world is watching—in a manner wholly unlike other impeachments. Most important, when senators oust a judge, they undo their own prior vote (via advice and consent to judicial nominees). When they remove a duly elected president, they undo the votes of millions of ordinary Americans on Election Day. This is not something that senators should do lightly, lest we slide toward a kind of parliamentary government that our entire structure of government was designed to repudiate."[70]

For a similar effort to ponder post-Founding presidential precedents, see Cass R. Sunstein, Impeaching the President, 147 U. Pa. L. Rev. 279 (1998). Sunstein concludes that "historical practice suggests a broader congressional power to impeach judges than presidents, and indeed, it suggests a special congressional reluctance to proceed against the President."[71]

8. Must the Senate remove a President who has committed a High Crime and Misdemeanor? Finally, assume that two-thirds of the Senators (or more) are convinced that the President has committed a high crime and misdemeanor. Must the Senate remove him from office, or does the Senate's decision also depend on larger political considerations? Consider the following structural argument:

[S]enators must . . . decide whether a given perjury warrants removal as a matter of sound judgment and statesmanship. In making this decision, they must be sensitive to the ways in which the presidency is a very different office from a federal district judgeship. Where extremely "high crimes" are implicated—treason or tyranny—senators should probably be quicker to pull the trigger on a bad president, whose office enables him unilaterally to do many dangerous things. (A single bad

70. Amar, Trial and Tribulation, The New Republic, Jan. 18, 1999. See also Tribe, supra:

[Even though Article II section 4 defines impeachable offenses for all federal officers], the Constitution nowhere mandates that the *definition* of a high crime be independent of the nature of the office from which it is proposed that someone be removed—independent for example, . . . of the mode of the office's selection (whether by the people in a national election, for example, or by the President with the concurrence of the Senate) . . . . [A judge may well be] removable for conduct that would not warrant removal of a president, particularly since Senate removal of a judge entails reversing the Senate's own action in confirming the judge whereas Senate removal of a president entails reversing an action of the entire national electorate.

71. With Amar and Sunstein, compare John O. McGinnis, Impeachment: The Structural Understanding, 67 Geo. Wash. L. Rev. 650, 660 (1999) (pointing to certain antipopulist features of the original Constitution, and rejecting the argument that the "legal standard for impeaching a President should be higher than the legal standard for impeaching a judge because the President has been elected by the people whereas a judge has been appointed. . . . .Indeed, important considerations of constitutional structure might well suggest the opposite conclusion, that we should be more loathe to retain a President in office who has breached the public trust than any other official, including a judge.").

judge, by contrast, is hemmed in by colleagues and higher courts.) But where borderline or low "high crimes" are involved, the Senate would be wise to spare the people's president—especially if his crimes reflect character flaws that the people duly considered before voting for him, or if the people continue to support him even after the facts come to light.

[Consider] Andrew Jackson, who killed a man in a duel before he was elected president. Technically, this was a crime, although it was rarely prosecuted in Jackson's day. Should Congress have impeached and removed Jackson even if the people who elected him knew about his crime and voted for him anyway? The duel Jackson fought concerned his wife's honor and chastity. Suppose Jackson had lied under oath to protect his wife's honor. Again, suppose the people knew all this when they voted for him. Should Congress have undone the people's votes on a theory that all crime is high crime, and that all perjury is the same?

Now consider the next presidential Andrew—Johnson, that is. Given our structural analysis, it seems relevant that Johnson was never elected president in his own right and that he was in fact working to undo the policies of the man the people did elect, Abraham Lincoln. If ever our structural argument cautioning restraint in ousting an elected president were weak, it was here, since Johnson lacked a genuine electoral mandate. And his policies toward unrepentant rebels could have been viewed as akin to treason, giving aid and comfort to men who were—not to mince words—traitors. And yet even here—an unelected president cozying up to actual traitors—the Senate acquitted.

Finally, consider President Nixon, whose extremely "high crimes" and gross abuses of official power posed a threat to our basic constitutional system. Although Nixon was elected by the people, his own unprecedented use of political espionage and sabotage tainted his mandate, in the same way that bribing electors would have. When all the facts were brought to light and the tapes came out, the people did indeed turn against him, prompting leaders of both parties to conclude that the time had come for him to go.[72]

How should this analysis apply to President Trump? Trump's lying, immorality, and unethical business practices were well known before he was elected. Trump lost the popular vote, and has been one of the more unpopular presidents in modern history. However, he has a devoted base of supporters, and his party has a majority in the Senate. Is his situation most like Jackson's, Johnson's, Nixon's, or none of the above?

Note: The Mueller Report

[President Trump fired FBI Director James Comey on May 9, 2017. Comey had been leading an FBI investigation into connections between Russia and various Trump associates and members of the Trump 2016 presidential campaign.

---

72. Amar, supra .

After Comey's dismissal, political pressure increased for a special counsel to investigate Russian interference in the 2016 election. On May 17, 2017, Deputy Attorney General Rod Rosenstein appointed Robert Mueller, a former FBI director, as a special counsel to conduct both a counter-intelligence investigation and a criminal investigation. On March 22, 2019, Mueller delivered his report on the criminal investigation to Attorney General William Barr. Barr, in turn, released a redacted version of the report to the public on April 18, 2019. Parts of the report are excerpted below.]

Report on the Investigation into Russian Interference in the 2016 Presidential Election

(The Mueller Report)

Executive Summary to Volume I

Russian Social Media Campaign

The Internet Research Agency (IRA) carried out the earliest Russian interference operations identified by the investigation—a social media campaign designed to provoke and amplify political and social discord in the United States. . . . The IRA later used social media accounts and interest groups to sow discord in the U.S. political system through what it termed "information warfare." The campaign evolved from a generalized program designed in 2014 and 2015 to undermine the U.S. electoral system, to a targeted operation that by early 2016 favored candidate Trump and disparaged candidate Clinton. The IRA's operation also included the purchase of political advertisements on social media in the names of U.S. persons and entities, as well as the staging of political rallies inside the United States. To organize those rallies, IRA employees posed as U.S. grassroots entities and persons and made contact with Trump supporters and Trump Campaign officials in the United States. The investigation did not identify evidence that any U.S. persons conspired or coordinated with the IRA. . . .

Russian Hacking Operations

At the same time that the IRA operation began to focus on supporting candidate Trump in early 2016, the Russian government employed a second form of interference: cyber intrusions (hacking) and releases of hacked materials damaging to the Clinton Campaign. The Russian intelligence service known as the Main Intelligence Directorate of the General Staff of the Russian Army (GRU) carried out these operations.

In March 2016, the GRU began hacking the email accounts of Clinton Campaign volunteers and employees, including campaign chairman John

Podesta. In April 2016, the GRU hacked into the computer networks of the Democratic Congressional Campaign Committee (DCCC) and the Democratic National Committee (DNC). The GRU stole hundreds of thousands of documents from the compromised email accounts and networks. Around the time that the DNC announced in mid-June 2016 the Russian government's role in hacking its network, the GRU began disseminating stolen materials through the fictitious online personas "DCLeaks" and "Guccifer 2.0." The GRU later released additional materials through the organization WikiLeaks.

The presidential campaign of Donald J. Trump ("Trump Campaign" or "Campaign") showed interest in WikiLeaks's releases of documents and welcomed their potential to damage candidate Clinton. Beginning in June 2016, [REDACTED] forecast to senior Campaign officials that WikiLeaks would release information damaging to candidate Clinton. WikiLeaks's first release came in July 2016. Around the same time, candidate Trump announced that he hoped Russia would recover emails described as missing from a private server used by Clinton when she was Secretary of State (he later said that he was speaking sarcastically). [REDACTED] WikiLeaks began releasing Podesta's stolen emails on October 7, 2016, less than one hour after a U.S. media outlet released [the Access Hollywood] video considered damaging to candidate Trump. Section III of this Report details the Office's investigation into the Russian hacking operations, as well as other efforts by Trump Campaign supporters to obtain Clinton-related emails.

Russian Contacts With The Campaign

The social media campaign and the GRU hacking operations coincided with a series of contacts between Trump Campaign officials and individuals with ties to the Russian government. The Office investigated whether those contacts reflected or resulted in the Campaign conspiring or coordinating with Russia in its election-interference activities. Although the investigation established that the Russian government perceived it would benefit from a Trump presidency and worked to secure that outcome, and that the Campaign expected it would benefit electorally from information stolen and released through Russian efforts, the investigation did not establish that members of the Trump Campaign conspired or coordinated with the Russian government in its election interference activities.

The Russian contacts consisted of business connections, offers of assistance to the Campaign, invitations for candidate Trump and Putin to meet in person, invitations for Campaign officials and representatives of the Russian government to meet, and policy positions seeking improved U.S.-Russian relations. . . .

Some of the earliest contacts were made in connection with a Trump Organization real-estate project in Russia known as Trump Tower Moscow. Candidate Trump signed a Letter of Intent for Trump Tower Moscow by November 2015, and in January 2016 Trump Organization executive Michael Cohen emailed and spoke about the project with the office of Russian government press secretary Dmitry Peskov. The Trump Organization pursued the project through at least June 2016, including by considering travel to Russia by Cohen and candidate Trump. . . .

Russian outreach to the Trump Campaign continued into the summer of 2016, as candidate Trump was becoming the presumptive Republican nominee for President. On June 9, 2016, for example, a Russian lawyer met with senior Trump Campaign officials Donald Trump Jr., Jared Kushner, and campaign chairman Paul Manafort to deliver what the email proposing the meeting had described as "official documents and information that would incriminate Hillary." The materials were offered to Trump Jr. as "part of Russia and its government's support for Mr. Trump." The written communications setting up the meeting showed that the Campaign anticipated receiving information from Russia that could assist candidate Trump's electoral prospects, but the Russian lawyer's presentation did not provide such information.

Days after the June 9 meeting, on June 14, 2016, a cybersecurity firm and the DNC announced that Russian government hackers had infiltrated the DNC and obtained access to opposition research on candidate Trump, among other documents. . . .

July 2016 was also the month WikiLeaks first released emails stolen by the GRU from the DNC. On July 22, 2016, WikiLeaks posted thousands of internal DNC documents revealing information about the Clinton Campaign . . . On October 7, 2016, the media released video of candidate Trump speaking in graphic terms about women years earlier, which was considered damaging to his candidacy. Less than an hour later, WikiLeaks made its second release: thousands of John Podesta's emails that had been stolen by the GRU in late March 2016. The FBI and other U.S. government institutions were at the time continuing their investigation of suspected Russian government efforts to interfere in the presidential election. That same day, October 7, the Department of Homeland Security and the Office of the Director of National Intelligence issued a joint public statement "that the Russian Government directed the recent compromises of e-mails from US persons and institutions, including from US political organizations." Those "thefts" and the "disclosures" of the hacked materials through online platforms such as WikiLeaks, the statement continued, "are intended to interfere with the US election process."

Immediately after the November 8 election, Russian government officials and prominent Russian businessmen began trying to make inroads into the new administration. The most senior levels of the Russian government encouraged these efforts. . . .

On December 29, 2016, then-President Obama imposed sanctions on Russia for having interfered in the election. Incoming National Security Advisor Michael Flynn called Russian Ambassador Sergey Kislyak and asked Russia not to escalate the situation in response to the sanctions. The following day, Putin announced that Russia would not take retaliatory measures in response to the sanctions at that time. Hours later, President-Elect Trump tweeted, "Great move on delay (by V. Putin)." The next day, on December 31, 2016, Kislyak called Flynn and told him the request had been received at the highest levels and Russia had chosen not to retaliate as a result of Flynn's request.

* * *

On January 6,2017, members of the intelligence community briefed President-Elect Trump on a joint assessment — drafted and coordinated among the Central Intelligence Agency, FBI, and National Security Agency — that concluded with high confidence that Russia had intervened in the election through a variety of means to assist Trump's candidacy and harm Clinton's. A declassified version of the assessment was publicly released that same day. . . . [In March 2017] Then-FBI Director James Comey later confirmed to Congress the existence of the FBI's investigation into Russian interference that had begun before the election. . . . The investigation continued under then-Director Comey for the next seven weeks until May 9, 2017, when President Trump fired Comey as FBI Director — an action which is analyzed in Volume II of the report.

On May 17,2017, Acting Attorney General Rod Rosenstein appointed the Special Counsel and authorized him to conduct the investigation that Comey had confirmed in his congressional testimony, as well as matters arising directly from the investigation, and any other matters within the scope of 28 C.F.R. § 600.4(a), which generally covers efforts to interfere with or obstruct the investigation.

President Trump reacted negatively to the Special Counsel's appointment. He told advisors that it was the end of his presidency, sought to have Attorney General Jefferson (Jeff) Sessions unrecuse from the Russia investigation and to have the Special Counsel removed, and engaged in efforts to curtail the Special Counsel's investigation and prevent the disclosure of evidence to it, including through public and private contacts with potential witnesses. Those and related actions are described and analyzed in Volume II of the report.

* * *

The Special Counsel's Charging Decisions

In reaching the charging decisions described in Volume I of the report, the Office determined whether the conduct it found amounted to a violation of federal criminal law chargeable under the Principles of Federal Prosecution. See Justice Manual § 9-27.000 et seq. (2018). The standard set forth in the Justice Manual is whether the conduct constitutes a crime; if so, whether admissible evidence would probably be sufficient to obtain and sustain a conviction; and whether prosecution would serve a substantial federal interest that could not be adequately served by prosecution elsewhere or through non-criminal alternatives. See Justice Manual § 9- 27.220. . . .

First, the Office determined that Russia's two principal interference operations in the 2016 U.S. presidential election — the social media campaign and the hacking-and-dumping operations — violated U.S. criminal law. . . .

Second, while the investigation identified numerous links between individuals with ties to the Russian government and individuals associated with the Trump Campaign, the evidence was not sufficient to support criminal charges. Among other things, the evidence was not sufficient to charge any Campaign official as an unregistered agent of the Russian government or other Russian principal. And our evidence about the June 9, 2016 meeting and WikiLeaks's releases of hacked materials was not sufficient to charge a criminal campaign-finance violation. Further, the evidence was not sufficient to charge that any member of the Trump Campaign conspired with representatives of the Russian government to interfere in the 2016 election.

Third, the investigation established that several individuals affiliated with the Trump Campaign lied to the Office, and to Congress, about their interactions with Russian-affiliated individuals and related matters. Those lies materially impaired the investigation of Russian election interference. The Office charged some of those lies as violations of the federal false- statements statute. Former National Security Advisor Michael Flynn pleaded guilty to lying about his interactions with Russian Ambassador Kislyak during the transition period. George Papadopoulos, a foreign policy advisor during the campaign period, pleaded guilty to lying to investigators about, inter alia, the nature and timing of his interactions with Joseph Mifsud, the professor who told Papadopoulos that the Russians had dirt on candidate Clinton in the form of thousands of emails. Former Trump Organization attorney Michael Cohen pleaded guilty to making false statements to Congress about the Trump Moscow project. [REDACTED] And in February 2019, the U.S. District Court for the District of Columbia found that Manafort lied to the Office and the grand jury concerning his interactions and communications with Konstantin Kilimnik about Trump Campaign polling data and a peace plan for Ukraine.

* * *

. . . The investigation did not always yield admissible information or testimony, or a complete picture of the activities undertaken by subjects of the investigation. Some individuals invoked their Fifth Amendment right against compelled self-incrimination and were not, in the Office's judgment, appropriate candidates for grants of immunity. The Office limited its pursuit of other witnesses and information—such as information known to attorneys or individuals claiming to be members of the media—in light of internal Department of Justice policies. See, e.g., Justice Manual §§ 9-13.400, 13.410. Some of the information obtained via court process, moreover, was presumptively covered by legal privilege and was screened from investigators by a filter (or "taint") team. Even when individuals testified or agreed to be interviewed, they sometimes provided information that was false or incomplete, leading to some of the false-statements charges described above. And the Office faced practical limits on its ability to access relevant evidence as well—numerous witnesses and subjects lived abroad, and documents were held outside the United States.

Further, the Office learned that some of the individuals we interviewed or whose conduct we investigated—including some associated with the Trump Campaign—deleted relevant communications or communicated during the relevant period using applications that feature encryption or that do not provide for long-term retention of data or communications records. In such cases, the Office was not able to corroborate witness statements through comparison to contemporaneous communications or fully question witnesses about statements that appeared inconsistent with other known facts.

Accordingly, while this report embodies factual and legal determinations that the Office believes to be accurate and complete to the greatest extent possible, given these identified gaps, the Office cannot rule out the possibility that the unavailable information would shed additional light on (or cast in a new light) the events described in the report.

. . . .

V. Prosecution and Declination Decisions

The Appointment Order authorized the Special Counsel's Office "to prosecute federal crimes arising from [its] investigation" of the matters assigned to it. In deciding whether to exercise this prosecutorial authority, the Office has been guided by the Principles of Federal Prosecution set forth in the Justice (formerly U.S. Attorney's) Manual. In particular, the Office has evaluated whether the conduct of the individuals considered for prosecution constituted a federal offense and whether admissible evidence would probably be sufficient to obtain and sustain a conviction for such an offense. Justice Manual § 9-27.220 (2018). Where the answer to those questions was yes, the Office further considered whether the prosecution would serve a substantial federal interest, the individuals were subject to effective prosecution in another jurisdiction, and there existed an adequate non-criminal alternative to prosecution. Id.

C. Russian Government Outreach and Contacts

. . . [T]he Office's investigation uncovered evidence of numerous links (i.e., contacts) between Trump Campaign officials and individuals having or claiming to have ties to the Russian government. . . . After considering the available evidence, the Office did not pursue charges under these statutes against any of the individuals . . . with the exception of FARA charges against Paul Manafort and Richard Gates based on their activities on behalf of Ukraine.

[T]he June 9, 2016 meeting between high-ranking campaign officials and Russians promising derogatory information on Hillary Clinton—implicates an additional body of law: campaign- finance statutes. Schemes involving the solicitation or receipt of assistance from foreign sources raise difficult statutory and constitutional questions. . . . The Office ultimately concluded that, even if the principal legal questions were resolved favorably to the government, a prosecution would encounter difficulties proving that Campaign officials or individuals connected to the Campaign willfully violated the law.

Finally, although the evidence of contacts between Campaign officials and Russia- affiliated individuals may not have been sufficient to establish or sustain criminal charges, several U.S. persons connected to the Campaign made false statements about those contacts and took other steps to obstruct the Office's investigation and those of Congress. This Office has therefore charged some of those individuals with making false statements and obstructing justice.

1. Potential Coordination: Conspiracy and Collusion

. . . [T]his Office evaluated potentially criminal conduct that involved the collective action of multiple individuals not under the rubric of "collusion," but through the lens of conspiracy law . . . In so doing, the Office recognized that the word "collud[e]" appears in the Acting Attorney General's August 2, 2017 memorandum; it has frequently been invoked in public reporting; and it is sometimes referenced in antitrust law, see, e.g., Brooke Group v. Brown & Williamson Tobacco Corp., 509 U.S. 209, 227 (1993). But collusion is not a specific offense or theory of liability found in the U.S. Code; nor is it a term of art in federal criminal law. To the contrary, even as defined in legal dictionaries, collusion is largely synonymous with conspiracy as that crime is set forth in the general federal conspiracy statute, 18 U.S.C. § 371. . . . For that reason, this Office's focus in resolving the question of joint criminal liability was on conspiracy as defined in federal law, not the commonly discussed term "collusion." . . . The investigation did not establish that the contacts described . . . amounted to an agreement to commit any substantive violation of federal criminal law — including foreign-influence and campaign-finance laws, both of which are discussed further below. The Office therefore did not charge any individual associated with the Trump Campaign with conspiracy to commit a federal offense arising from Russia contacts. . . .

The investigation did not establish any agreement among Campaign officials — or between such officials and Russia-linked individuals — to interfere with or obstruct a lawful function of a government agency during the campaign or transition period. And, . . . the investigation did not identify evidence that any Campaign official or associate knowingly and intentionally participated in the conspiracy to defraud that the Office charged, namely, the [Russia-backed] active-measures conspiracy [to use social media to influence the election] . . . Accordingly, the Office did not charge any Campaign associate or other U.S. person with conspiracy to defraud the United States based on the Russia-related contacts . . .

2. Potential Coordination: Foreign Agent Statutes (FARA and 18 U.S.C. § 951)

. . . Under 18 U.S.C. § 951, it is generally illegal to act in the United States as an agent of a foreign government without providing notice to the Attorney General. Although the defendant must act on behalf of a foreign government (as opposed to other kinds of foreign entities), the acts need not involve espionage;

rather, acts of any type suffice for liability. . . . The crime defined by Section 951 is complete upon knowingly acting in the United States as an unregistered foreign-government agent. 18 U.S.C. § 951(a). The statute does not require willfulness, and knowledge of the notification requirement is not an element of the offense. . . .

The investigation uncovered extensive evidence that Paul Manafort's and Richard Gates's pre-campaign work for the government of Ukraine violated FARA. . . . The investigation did not, however, yield evidence sufficient to sustain any charge that any individual affiliated with the Trump Campaign acted as an agent of a foreign principal within the meaning of FARA or, in terms of Section 951, subject to the direction or control of the government of Russia, or any official thereof. In particular, the Office did not find evidence likely to prove beyond a reasonable doubt that Campaign officials such as Paul Manafort, George Papadopoulos, and Carter Page acted as agents of the Russian government—or at its direction, control, or request—during the relevant time period. . . .

3. Campaign Finance

. . . "[T]he United States has a compelling interest . . . in limiting the participation of foreign citizens in activities of democratic self-government, and in thereby preventing foreign influence over the U.S. political process." Bluman v. FEC, 800 F. Supp. 2d 281, 288 (D.D.C. 2011) (Kavanaugh, J., for three-judge court), affd, 565 U.S. 1104 (2012). To that end, federal campaign- finance law broadly prohibits foreign nationals from making contributions, donations, expenditures, or other disbursements in connection with federal, state, or local candidate elections, and prohibits anyone from soliciting, accepting, or receiving such contributions or donations. As relevant here, foreign nationals may not make—and no one may "solicit, accept, or receive" from them—"a contribution or donation of money or other thing of value" or "an express or implied promise to make a contribution or donation, in connection with a Federal, State, or local election." 52 U.S.C. § 30121(a)(1)(A), (a)(2). The term "contribution," which is used throughout the campaign-finance law, "includes" "any gift, subscription, loan, advance, or deposit of money or anything of value made by any person for the purpose of influencing any election for Federal office." 52 U.S.C. § 30101 (8)(A)(i). It excludes, among other things, "the value of [volunteer] services." 52 U.S.C. § 30101(8)(B)(i).

Foreign nationals are also barred from making "an expenditure, independent expenditure, or disbursement for an electioneering communication." 52 U.S.C. § 30121(a)(1)(C). The term "expenditure" "includes" "any purchase, payment, distribution, loan, advance, deposit, or gift of money or anything of value, made by any person for the purpose of influencing any election for Federal office." 52 U.S.C. § 30101 (9)(A)(i). It excludes, among other things, news stories and nonpartisan get-out-the-vote activities. 52 U.S.C. § 30101 (9)(B)(i)-(ii). An "independent expenditure" is an expenditure "expressly advocating the election or defeat of a clearly identified candidate" and made independently of the campaign.

52 U.S.C. § 30101(17). An "electioneering communication" is a broadcast communication that "refers to a clearly identified candidate for Federal office" and is made within specified time periods and targeted at the relevant electorate. 52 U.S.C. § 30104(f)(3). . . .

The Office considered whether to charge Trump Campaign officials with crimes in connection with the June 9 [Trump Tower] meeting . . . The Office concluded that, in light of the government's substantial burden of proof on issues of intent ("knowing" and "willful"), and the difficulty of establishing the value of the offered information, criminal charges would not meet the Justice Manual standard that "the admissible evidence will probably be sufficient to obtain and sustain a conviction." Justice Manual § 9-27.220.

In brief, the key facts are that, on June 3, 2016, Robert Goldstone emailed Donald Trump Jr., to pass along from Emin and Aras Agalarov an "offer" from Russia's "Crown prosecutor" to "the Trump campaign" of "official documents and information that would incriminate Hillary and her dealings with Russia and would be very useful to [Trump Jr.'s] father." The email described this as "very high level and sensitive information" that is "part of Russia and its government's support to Mr. Trump-helped along by Aras and Emin." Trump Jr. responded: "if it's what you say I love it especially later in the summer." Trump Jr. and Emin Agalarov had follow-up conversations and, within days, scheduled a meeting with Russian representatives that was attended by Trump Jr., Manafort, and Kushner. The communications setting up the meeting and the attendance by high-level Campaign representatives support an inference that the Campaign anticipated receiving derogatory documents and information from official Russian sources that could assist candidate Trump's electoral prospects.

This series of events could implicate the federal election-law ban on contributions and donations by foreign nationals, 52 U.S.C. § 30121(a)(1)(A). Specifically, Goldstone passed along an offer purportedly from a Russian government official to provide "official documents and information" to the Trump Campaign for the purposes of influencing the presidential election. Trump Jr. appears to have accepted that offer and to have arranged a meeting to receive those materials. Documentary evidence in the form of email chains supports the inference that Kushner and Manafort were aware of that purpose and attended the June 9 meeting anticipating the receipt of helpful information to the Campaign from Russian sources.

The Office considered whether this evidence would establish a conspiracy to violate the foreign contributions ban, in violation of 18 U.S.C. § 371; the solicitation of an illegal foreign- source contribution; or the acceptance or receipt of "an express or implied promise to make a [foreign-source] contribution," both in violation of 52 U.S.C. § 30121(a)(1)(A), (a)(2). There are reasonable arguments that the offered information would constitute a "thing of value" within the meaning of these provisions, but the Office determined that the government would not be likely to obtain and sustain a conviction for two other reasons: first, the Office did not obtain admissible evidence likely to meet the government's burden to prove beyond a reasonable doubt that these individuals acted "willfully," i.e., with general knowledge of the illegality of their conduct; and, second, the government would likely encounter difficulty in proving beyond a reasonable doubt that the value of the promised information exceeded the threshold for a criminal violation. . . .

Federal Election Commission (FEC) regulations [and opinions] . . . would support the view that candidate-related opposition research given to a campaign for the purpose of influencing an election could constitute a contribution to which the foreign-source ban could apply. A campaign can be assisted not only by the provision of funds, but also by the provision of derogatory information about an opponent. Political campaigns frequently conduct and pay for opposition research. A foreign entity that engaged in such research and provided resulting information to a campaign could exert a greater effect on an election, and a greater tendency to ingratiate the donor to the candidate, than a gift of money or tangible things of value. At the same time, no judicial decision has treated the voluntary provision of uncompensated opposition research or similar information as a thing of value that could amount to a contribution under campaign-finance law. Such an interpretation could have implications beyond the foreign-source ban, see 52 U.S.C. § 30116(a) (imposing monetary limits on campaign contributions), and raise First Amendment questions. Those questions could be especially difficult where the information consisted simply of the recounting of historically accurate facts. It is uncertain how courts would resolve those issues. . . .

[In addition,] [T]he government has not obtained admissible evidence that is likely to establish the scienter requirement beyond a reasonable doubt. To prove that a defendant acted "knowingly and willfully," the government would have to show that the defendant had general knowledge that his conduct was unlawful. . . . U.S. Department of Justice, Federal Prosecution of Election Offenses 123 (8th ed. Dec. 2017) ("Election Offenses") . . . "This standard creates an elevated scienter element requiring, at the very least, that application of the law to the facts in question be fairly clear. When there is substantial doubt concerning whether the law applies to the facts of a particular matter, the offender is more likely to have an intent defense." Election Offenses 123.

On the facts here, the government would unlikely be able to prove beyond a reasonable doubt that the June 9 meeting participants had general knowledge that their conduct was unlawful. The investigation has not developed evidence that the participants in the meeting were familiar with the foreign-contribution ban or the application of federal law to the relevant factual context. The government does not have strong evidence of surreptitious behavior or efforts at concealment at the time of the June 9 meeting. While the government has evidence of later efforts to prevent disclosure of the nature of the June 9 meeting that could circumstantially provide support for a showing of scienter [which is described in Volume II of the report on issues of obstruction of justice] . . . that concealment occurred more than a year later, involved individuals who did not attend the June 9 meeting, and may reflect an intention to avoid political consequences rather than any prior knowledge of illegality. Additionally, in light of the unresolved legal questions about whether giving "documents and information" of the sort offered here constitutes a campaign contribution, Trump Jr. could mount a factual defense that he did not believe his response to the offer and the June 9 meeting itself violated the law. Given his less direct involvement in arranging the June 9 meeting, Kushner could likely mount a similar defense. And, while Manafort is experienced with political campaigns, the Office has not developed evidence showing that he had relevant knowledge of these legal issues.

iii. Difficulties in Valuing Promised Information

The Office would also encounter difficulty proving beyond a reasonable doubt that the value of the promised documents and information exceeds the $2,000 threshold for a criminal violation, as well as the $25,000 threshold for felony punishment. See 52 U.S.C. § 30109(d)(1). . . . Although damaging opposition research is surely valuable to a campaign, it appears that the information ultimately delivered in the meeting was not valuable. And while value in a conspiracy may well be measured by what the participants expected to receive at the time of the agreement, . . . Goldstone's description of the offered material here was quite general. His suggestion of the information's value — i.e., that it would "incriminate Hillary" and "would be very useful to [Trump Jr.'s] father" — was nonspecific and may have been understood as being of uncertain worth or reliability, given Goldstone's lack of direct access to the original source. The uncertainty over what would be delivered could be reflected in Trump Jr.'s response ("if it's what you say I love it"). . . .

Accordingly, taking into account the high burden to establish a culpable mental state in a campaign-finance prosecution and the difficulty in establishing the required valuation, the Office decided not to pursue criminal campaign-finance charges against Trump Jr. or other campaign officials for the events culminating in the June 9 meeting.

Introduction to Volume II

. . . Beginning in 2017, the President of the United States took a variety of actions towards the ongoing FBI investigation into Russia's interference in the 2016 presidential election and related matters that raised questions about whether he had obstructed justice. The Order appointing the Special Counsel gave this Office jurisdiction to investigate matters that arose directly from the FBI's Russia investigation, including whether the President had obstructed justice in connection with Russia-related investigations. The Special Counsel's jurisdiction also covered potentially obstructive acts related to the Special Counsel's investigation itself. This Volume of our report summarizes our obstruction-of-justice investigation of the President. . . .

First, a traditional prosecution or declination decision entails a binary determination to initiate or decline a prosecution, but we determined not to make a traditional prosecutorial judgment. The Office of Legal Counsel (OLC) has issued an opinion finding that "the indictment or criminal prosecution of a sitting President would impermissibly undermine the capacity of the executive branch to perform its constitutionally assigned functions" in violation of "the constitutional separation of powers." [A Sitting President's Amenability to Indictment and Criminal Prosecution, 24 Op. O.L.C. 222, 222, 260 (2000) (OLC Op.).] Given the role of the Special Counsel as an attorney in the Department of Justice and the framework of the Special Counsel regulations, see 28 U.S.C. § 515; 28 C.F.R. § 600.7(a), this Office accepted OLC's legal conclusion for the purpose of exercising prosecutorial jurisdiction. And apart from OLC's constitutional view, we recognized that a federal criminal accusation against a sitting President would place burdens on the President's capacity to govern and potentially preempt constitutional processes for addressing presidential misconduct.

Second, while the OLC opinion concludes that a sitting President may not be prosecuted, it recognizes that a criminal investigation during the President's term is permissible. The OLC opinion also recognizes that a President does not have immunity after he leaves office. And if individuals other than the President committed an obstruction offense, they may be prosecuted at this time. Given those considerations, the facts known to us, and the strong public interest in safeguarding the integrity of the criminal justice system, we conducted a thorough factual investigation in order to preserve the evidence when memories were fresh and documentary materials were available.

Third, we considered whether to evaluate the conduct we investigated under the Justice Manual standards governing prosecution and declination decisions, but we determined not to apply an approach that could potentially result in a judgment that the President committed crimes. The threshold step under the Justice Manual standards is to assess whether a person's conduct "constitutes a federal offense." U.S. Dep't of Justice, Justice Manual § 9-27.220 (2018) (Justice Manual). Fairness concerns counseled against potentially reaching that judgment when no charges can be brought. The ordinary means for an individual to respond to an accusation is through a speedy and public trial, with all the procedural protections that surround a criminal case. An individual who believes he was wrongly accused can use that process to seek to clear his name. In contrast, a prosecutor's judgment that crimes were committed, but that no charges will be brought, affords no such adversarial opportunity for public name-clearing before an impartial adjudicator.

The concerns about the fairness of such a determination would be heightened in the case of a sitting President, where a federal prosecutor's accusation of a crime, even in an internal report, could carry consequences that extend beyond the realm of criminal justice. OLC noted similar concerns about sealed indictments. Even if an indictment were sealed during the President's term, OLC reasoned, "it would be very difficult to preserve [an indictment's] secrecy," and if an indictment became public, "[t]he stigma and opprobrium" could imperil the President's ability to govern." Although a prosecutor's internal report would not represent a formal public accusation akin to an indictment, the possibility of the report's public disclosure and the absence of a neutral adjudicatory forum to review its findings counseled against potentially determining "that the person's conduct constitutes a federal offense." Justice Manual § 9-27.220.

Fourth, if we had confidence after a thorough investigation of the facts that the President clearly did not commit obstruction of justice, we would so state. Based on the facts and the applicable legal standards, however, we are unable to reach that judgment. The evidence we obtained about the President's actions and intent presents difficult issues that prevent us from conclusively determining that no criminal conduct occurred. Accordingly, while this report does not conclude that the President committed a crime, it also does not exonerate him. . . .

Factual Results of the Obstruction Investigation

The key issues and events we examined include the following:

The Campaign's response to reports about Russian support for Trump. During the 2016 presidential campaign, questions arose about the Russian government's apparent support for candidate Trump. After WikiLeaks released politically damaging Democratic Party emails that were reported to have been hacked by Russia, Trump publicly expressed skepticism that Russia was responsible for the hacks at the same time that he and other Campaign officials privately sought information [REDACTED] about any further planned WikiLeaks releases. Trump also denied having any business in or connections to Russia, even though as late as June 2016 the Trump Organization had been pursuing a licensing deal for a skyscraper to be built in Russia called Trump Tower Moscow. After the election, the President expressed concerns to advisors that reports of Russia's election interference might lead the public to question the legitimacy of his election.

Conduct involving FBI Director Comey and Michael Flynn. In mid-January 2017, incoming National Security Advisor Michael Flynn falsely denied to the Vice President, other administration officials, and FBI agents that he had talked to Russian Ambassador Sergey Kislyak about Russia's response to U.S. sanctions on Russia for its election interference. On January 27, the day after the President was told that Flynn had lied to the Vice President and had made similar statements to the FBI, the President invited FBI Director Comey to a private dinner at the White House and told Comey that he needed loyalty. On February 14, the day after the President requested Flynn's resignation, the President told an outside advisor, "Now that we fired Flynn, the Russia thing is over." The advisor disagreed and said the investigations would continue.

Later that afternoon, the President cleared the Oval Office to have a one-on-one meeting with Comey. Referring to the FBI's investigation of Flynn, the President said, "I hope you can see your way clear to letting this go, to letting Flynn go. He is a good guy. I hope you can let this go." Shortly after requesting

Flynn's resignation and speaking privately to Comey, the President sought to
have Deputy National Security Advisor K.T. McFarland draft an internal letter stating that the President had not directed Flynn to discuss sanctions with
Kislyak. McFarland declined because she did not know whether that was true,
and a White House Counsel's Office attorney thought that the request would
look like a quid pro quo for an ambassadorship she had been offered.

   The President's reaction to the continuing Russia investigation. In February
2017, Attorney General Jeff Sessions began to assess whether he had to recuse
himself from campaign- related investigations because of his role in the Trump
Campaign. In early March, the President told White House Counsel Donald
McGahn to stop Sessions from recusing. And after Sessions announced his recusal on March 2, the President expressed anger at the decision and told advisors
that he should have an Attorney General who would protect him. That weekend,
the President took Sessions aside at an event and urged him to "unrecuse." Later
in March, Comey publicly disclosed at a congressional hearing that the FBI was
investigating "the Russian government's efforts to interfere in the 2016 presidential election," including any links or coordination between the Russian government and the Trump Campaign. In the following days, the President reached out
to the Director of National Intelligence and the leaders of the Central Intelligence
Agency (CIA) and the National Security Agency (NSA) to ask them what they
could do to publicly dispel the suggestion that the President had any connection to the Russian election-interference effort. The President also twice called
Comey directly, notwithstanding guidance from McGahn to avoid direct contacts
with the Department of Justice. Comey had previously assured the President that
the FBI was not investigating him personally, and the President asked Comey to
"lift the cloud" of the Russia investigation by saying that publicly.

   The President's termination of Comey. On May 3, 2017, Comey testified
in a congressional hearing, but declined to answer questions about whether the
President was personally under investigation. Within days, the President decided
to terminate Comey. The President insisted that the termination letter, which was
written for public release, state that Comey had informed the President that he
was not under investigation. The day of the firing, the White House maintained
that Comey's termination resulted from independent recommendations from the
Attorney General and Deputy Attorney General that Comey should be discharged
for mishandling the Hillary Clinton email investigation. But the President had
decided to fire Comey before hearing from the Department of Justice. The day
after firing Comey, the President told Russian officials that he had "faced great
pressure because of Russia," which had been "taken off" by Comey's firing. The
next day, the President acknowledged in a television interview that he was going
to fire Comey regardless of the Department of Justice's recommendation and
that when he "decided to just do it," he was thinking that "this thing with Trump
and Russia is a made-up story." In response to a question about whether he was
angry with Comey about the Russia investigation, the President said, "As far as

I'm concerned, I want that thing to be absolutely done properly," adding that firing Comey "might even lengthen out the investigation."

The appointment of a Special Counsel and efforts to remove him. On May 17, 2017, the Acting Attorney General for the Russia investigation appointed a Special Counsel to conduct the investigation and related matters. The President reacted to news that a Special Counsel had been appointed by telling advisors that it was "the end of his presidency" and demanding that Sessions resign. Sessions submitted his resignation, but the President ultimately did not accept it. The President told aides that the Special Counsel had conflicts of interest and suggested that the Special Counsel therefore could not serve. The President's advisors told him the asserted conflicts were meritless and had already been considered by the Department of Justice.

On June 14, 2017, the media reported that the Special Counsel's Office was investigating whether the President had obstructed justice. Press reports called this "a major turning point" in the investigation: while Comey had told the President he was not under investigation, following Comey's firing, the President now was under investigation. The President reacted to this news with a series of tweets criticizing the Department of Justice and the Special Counsel's investigation. On June 17, 2017, the President called McGahn at home and directed him to call the Acting Attorney General and say that the Special Counsel had conflicts of interest and must be removed. McGahn did not carry out the direction, however, deciding that he would resign rather than trigger what he regarded as a potential Saturday Night Massacre.

Efforts to curtail the Special Counsel's investigation. Two days after directing McGahn to have the Special Counsel removed, the President made another attempt to affect the course of the Russia investigation. On June 19, 2017, the President met one-on-one in the Oval Office with his former campaign manager Corey Lewandowski, a trusted advisor outside the government, and dictated a message for Lewandowski to deliver to Sessions. The message said that Sessions should publicly announce that, notwithstanding his recusal from the Russia investigation, the investigation was "very unfair" to the President, the President had done nothing wrong, and Sessions planned to meet with the Special Counsel and "let [him] move forward with investigating election meddling for future elections." Lewandowski said he understood what the President wanted Sessions to do.

One month later, in another private meeting with Lewandowski on July 19, 2017, the President asked about the status of his message for Sessions to limit the Special Counsel investigation to future election interference. Lewandowski told the President that the message would be delivered soon. Hours after that meeting, the President publicly criticized Sessions in an interview with the New York Times, and then issued a series of tweets making it clear that Sessions's job was in jeopardy. Lewandowski did not want to deliver the President's message personally, so he asked senior White House official Rick Dearborn to deliver it to Sessions. Dearborn was uncomfortable with the task and did not follow through.

Efforts to prevent public disclosure of evidence. In the summer of 2017, the President learned that media outlets were asking questions about the June 9, 2016 meeting at Trump Tower between senior campaign officials, including Donald Trump Jr., and a Russian lawyer who was said to be offering damaging information about Hillary Clinton as "part of Russia and its government's support for Mr. Trump." On several occasions, the President directed aides not to publicly disclose the emails setting up the June 9 meeting, suggesting that the emails would not leak and that the number of lawyers with access to them should be limited. Before the emails became public, the President edited a press statement for Trump Jr. by deleting a line that acknowledged that the meeting was with "an individual who [Trump Jr.] was told might have information helpful to the campaign" and instead said only that the meeting was about adoptions of Russian children. When the press asked questions about the President's involvement in Trump Jr.'s statement, the President's personal lawyer repeatedly denied the President had played any role.

Further efforts to have the Attorney General take control of the investigation. In early summer 2017, the President called Sessions at home and again asked him to reverse his recusal from the Russia investigation. Sessions did not reverse his recusal. In October 2017, the President met privately with Sessions in the Oval Office and asked him to "take [a] look" at investigating Clinton. In December 2017, shortly after Flynn pleaded guilty pursuant to a cooperation agreement, the President met with Sessions in the Oval Office and suggested, according to notes taken by a senior advisor, that if Sessions unrecused and took back supervision of the Russia investigation, he would be a "hero." The President told Sessions, "I'm not going to do anything or direct you to do anything. I just want to be treated fairly." In response, Sessions volunteered that he had never seen anything "improper" on the campaign and told the President there was a "whole new leadership team" in place. He did not unrecuse.

Efforts to have McGahn deny that the President had ordered him to have the Special Counsel removed. In early 2018, the press reported that the President had directed McGahn to have the Special Counsel removed in June 2017 and that McGahn had threatened to resign rather than cany out the order. The President reacted to the news stories by directing White House officials to tell McGahn to dispute the story and create a record stating he had not been ordered to have the Special Counsel removed. McGahn told those officials that the media reports were accurate in stating that the President had directed McGahn to have the Special Counsel removed. The President then met with McGahn in the Oval Office and again pressured him to deny the reports. In the same meeting, the President also asked McGahn why he had told the Special Counsel about the President's effort to remove the Special Counsel and why McGahn took notes of his conversations with the President. McGahn refused to back away from what he remembered happening and perceived the President to be testing his mettle.

Conduct towards Flynn, Manafort, [REDACTED]. After Flynn withdrew from a joint defense agreement with the President and began cooperating with the government, the President's personal counsel left a message for Flynn's attorneys reminding them of the President's warm feelings towards Flynn, which he said "still remains," and asking for a "heads up" if Flynn knew "information that implicates the President." When Flynn's counsel reiterated that Flynn could no longer share information pursuant to a joint defense agreement, the President's personal counsel said he would make sure that the President knew that Flynn's actions reflected "hostility" towards the President. During Manafort's prosecution and when the jury in his criminal trial was deliberating, the President praised Manafort in public, said that Manafort was being treated unfairly, and declined to rule out a pardon. After Manafort was convicted, the President called Manafort "a brave man" for refusing to "break" and said that "flipping" "almost ought to be [REDACTED].

Conduct involving Michael Cohen. The President's conduct towards Michael Cohen, a former Trump Organization executive, changed from praise for Cohen when he falsely minimized the President's involvement in the Trump Tower Moscow project, to castigation of Cohen when he became a cooperating witness. From September 2015 to June 2016, Cohen had pursued the Trump Tower Moscow project on behalf of the Trump Organization and had briefed candidate Trump on the project numerous times, including discussing whether Trump should travel to Russia to advance the deal. In 2017, Cohen provided false testimony to Congress about the project, including stating that he had only briefed Trump on the project three times and never discussed travel to Russia with him, in an effort to adhere to a "party line" that Cohen said was developed to minimize the President's connections to Russia. While preparing for his congressional testimony, Cohen had extensive discussions with the President's personal counsel, who, according to Cohen, said that Cohen should "stay on message" and not contradict the President. After the FBI searched Cohen's home and office in April 2018, the President publicly asserted that Cohen would not "flip," contacted him directly to tell him to "stay strong," and privately passed messages of support to him. Cohen also discussed pardons with the President's personal counsel and believed that if he stayed on message he would be taken care of. But after Cohen began cooperating with the government in the summer of 2018, the President publicly criticized him, called him a "rat," and suggested that his family members had committed crimes.

Overarching factual issues. We did not make a traditional prosecution decision about these facts, but the evidence we obtained supports several general statements about the President's conduct.

Several features of the conduct we investigated distinguish it from typical obstruction-of- justice cases. First, the investigation concerned the President, and some of his actions, such as firing the FBI director, involved facially lawful acts within his Article II authority, which raises constitutional issues discussed below. At the same time, the President's position as the head of the Executive Branch provided him with unique and powerful means of influencing official proceedings, subordinate officers, and potential witnesses—all of which is relevant to a potential obstruction-of-justice analysis. Second, unlike cases in which a subject engages in obstruction of justice to cover up a crime, the evidence we obtained did not establish that the President was involved in an underlying crime related to Russian election interference. Although the obstruction statutes do not require proof of such a crime, the absence of that evidence affects the analysis of the President's intent and requires consideration of other possible motives for his conduct. Third, many of the President's acts directed at witnesses, including discouragement of cooperation with the government and suggestions of possible future pardons, took place in public view. That circumstance is unusual, but no principle of law excludes public acts from the reach of the obstruction laws. If the likely effect of public acts is to influence witnesses or alter their testimony, the harm to the justice system's integrity is the same.

Although the series of events we investigated involved discrete acts, the overall pattern of the President's conduct towards the investigations can shed light on the nature of the President's acts and the inferences that can be drawn about his intent. In particular, the actions we investigated can be divided into two phases, reflecting a possible shift in the President's motives. The first phase covered the period from the President's first interactions with Comey through the President's firing of Comey. During that time, the President had been repeatedly told he was not personally under investigation. Soon after the firing of Comey and the appointment of the Special Counsel, however, the President became aware that his own conduct was being investigated in an obstruction-of-justice inquiry. At that point, the President engaged in a second phase of conduct, involving public attacks on the investigation, non-public efforts to control it, and efforts in both public and private to encourage witnesses not to cooperate with the investigation. Judgments about the nature of the President's motives during each phase would be informed by the totality of the evidence.

. . . .

Constitutional defenses. As for constitutional defenses arising from the President's status as the head of the Executive Branch, we recognized that the Department of Justice and the courts have not definitively resolved these issues. We therefore examined those issues through the framework established by Supreme Court precedent governing separation-of-powers issues. The Department of Justice and the President's personal counsel have recognized that the President is subject to statutes that prohibit obstruction of justice by bribing a witness or suborning perjury because that conduct does not implicate his constitutional authority. With respect to whether the President can be found to have obstructed justice by exercising his powers under Article II of the Constitution, we concluded that Congress has authority to prohibit a President's corrupt use of his authority in order to protect the integrity of the administration of justice.

Under applicable Supreme Court precedent, the Constitution does not categorically and permanently immunize a President for obstructing justice through the use of his Article II powers. The separation-of-powers doctrine authorizes Congress to protect official proceedings, including those of courts and grand juries, from corrupt, obstructive acts regardless of their source. We also concluded that any inroad on presidential authority that would occur from prohibiting corrupt acts does not undermine the President's ability to fulfill his constitutional mission. The term "corruptly" sets a demanding standard. It requires a concrete showing that a person acted with an intent to obtain an improper advantage for himself or someone else, inconsistent with official duty and the rights of others. A preclusion of "corrupt" official action does not diminish the President's ability to exercise Article II powers. For example, the proper supervision of criminal law does not demand freedom for the President to act with a corrupt intention of shielding himself from criminal punishment, avoiding financial liability, or preventing personal embarrassment. To the contrary, a statute that prohibits official action undertaken for such corrupt purposes furthers, rather than hinders, the impartial and even-handed administration of the law. It also aligns with the President's constitutional duty to faithfully execute the laws. Finally, we concluded that in the rare case in which a criminal investigation of the President's conduct is justified, inquiries to determine whether the President acted for a corrupt motive should not impermissibly chill his performance of his constitutionally assigned duties. The conclusion that Congress may apply the obstruction laws to the President's corrupt exercise of the powers of office accords with our constitutional system of checks and balances and the principle that no person is above the law.

Conclusion

Because we determined not to make a traditional prosecutorial judgment, we did not draw ultimate conclusions about the President's conduct. The evidence we obtained about the President's actions and intent presents difficult issues that would need to be resolved if we were making a traditional prosecutorial judgment. At the same time, if we had confidence after a thorough investigation of the facts that the President clearly did not commit obstruction of justice, we would so state. Based on the facts and the applicable legal standards, we are unable to reach that judgment. Accordingly, while this report does not conclude that the President committed a crime, it also does not exonerate him.

Discussion

1. *Independent Counsel vs. Special Counsel.* When Kenneth Starr issued his report about President Clinton in 1998, it was immediately made conveyed to Congress and the public and was a national best seller. Starr also made referrals concerning possible grounds for impeachment to Congress. When the Mueller

report was completed in March 2019, by contrast, it was sent to Attorney General William Barr, who initially kept it confidential and issued a short summary and interpretation of its findings. The report was released in a redacted form to the public on April, 18, 2019. It contained no suggestions about impeachment.

Why the differences? Ken Starr was an independent counsel acting under the (since repealed) Independent Counsel Act. Congress enacted the ICA after the Watergate scandal; it was designed to prevent a repetition of the infamous "Saturday Night Massacre" of October 20, 1973—in which President Nixon ordered the firing of Watergate Special Prosecutor Archibald Cox. The ICA required the independent counsel to report to Congress to enable congressional oversight.

By contrast, Robert Mueller was a special counsel operating under Justice Department regulations adopted by the Clinton Justice Department after Clinton's impeachment. These regulations impose minimal reporting obligations on the special counsel. The Justice Department must advise Congress of the appointment or removal of a special counsel; and "[u]pon conclusion of the Special Counsel[']s investigation, including, to the extent consistent with applicable law, a description and explanation of instances (if any) in which the Attorney General concluded that a proposed action by a Special Counsel was so inappropriate or unwarranted under established Departmental practices that it should not be pursued." 28 C.F.R. 600.9 (a)(3).[73]

Ken Starr, the Independent Counsel in the Clinton investigation, explained the purpose for these differences between the ICA and the Justice Department regulations:

> The regulations now governing Mueller were meant to restore the traditions of the Department of Justice, which were broken when Congress enacted the special-prosecutor (or, later, independent-counsel) provisions of the Ethics in Government Act of 1978. Under that regime, reports became the warp and woof of the independent counsel's work. Most provocatively, the statute required an independent counsel to refer matters to the House of Representatives for possible impeachment when a surprisingly low threshold of evidence was in hand—"substantial and credible information that an impeachable offense may have been committed." I followed that requirement when I produced the so-called Starr Report, which then took on a controversial life of its own in the House in the dramatic months of 1998.
>
> The architects of the current regulations saw all this unfold. Not surprisingly, the drafters of the new regime—the one under which Mueller operates—set themselves firmly against the revolutionary principle of factually rich prosecutorial reports. It might seem strange for me to say, but they were right to do so. The message emanating from the new regulations, issued by then–Attorney General Janet Reno, was this: Special counsel, do your job, and then inform the attorney

---

73. See Cynthia Brown, The Special Counsel's Report: What Do Current DOJ Regulations Require?, Congressional Research Service, March 7, 2019, at https://fas.org/sgp/crs/misc/LSB10270.pdf

general — in confidence — of the reasons underlying your decisions to prosecute and your determinations not to seek a prosecution ("declinations").[74]

Because the Starr report was written to be released to the public, it omitted sensitive information and information about grand jury proceedings. Because the Mueller Report was written for the Attorney General, the Attorney General redacted information he believed should not be disclosed before releasing the report to the public.

The Special Counsel regulations reflected a concern about the separation of powers and the fact that the Special Counsel worked for the Justice Department, and, ultimately, the President. Is there any danger that the Attorney General — who also works for the President — will refuse to disclose important information to Congress that would hinder Congress's ability to decide whether impeachment is warranted? Is there any danger that the Attorney General will "spin" the report so that the public mistakenly believes that the President has been exonerated?

In fact, Attorney General Barr's initial summary of the report on March 24, 2019 was later criticized for misleading the public about the report's conclusions; nevertheless, the Attorney General released a redacted version of the report a month later.[75] Would altering the existing reporting requirements to require prompt disclosure to Congress be a good idea? Would it violate the separation of powers?

2. *The DOJ's position on prosecuting the President.* Special Counsel Mueller's report was shaped by the fact that, as an employee of the DOJ, he was bound by the DOJ's view that the Constitution does not permit criminal proceedings against a sitting president. Even if one disagrees with this judgment about the Constitution, Mueller was unlikely to act contrary to the views of his employer, regardless of his views on whether the President had engaged in criminal activity.

At a news conference on May 29, Mueller explained that "if we had had confidence that the president clearly did not commit a crime, we would have said so. We did not, however, make a determination as to whether the president did commit a crime. The introduction to the volume two of our report explains that decision. It explains that under long-standing department policy, a president cannot be charged with a federal crime while he is in office. That is unconstitutional. Even if the charge is kept under seal and hidden from public view, that, too, is prohibited. The special counsel's office is part of the Department of Justice and

74. Ken Starr, Mueller Cannot Seek an Indictment. And He Must Remain Silent, The Atlantic, March 22, 2019, https://www.theatlantic.com/ideas/archive/2019/03/ken-starr-muellers-report-shouldnt-go-congress/585577/

75. Mark Mazzetti and Michael S. Schmidt, Mueller Objected to Barr's Description of Russia Investigation's Findings on Trump, New York Times, April 30, 2019, https://www.nytimes.com/2019/04/30/us/politics/mueller-barr.html ; Ryan Goodman, A Side-by-Side Comparison of Barr's vs. Mueller's Statements about Special Counsel Report, Just Security, June 5, 2019, https://www.justsecurity.org/64441/a-side-by-side-comparison-of-barrs-vs-muellers-statements-about-special-counsel-report/ .

by regulation, it was bound by that department policy. Charging the president with a crime was therefore not an option we could consider."[76]

What, if anything, should be inferred from this statement?

3. *An ineffective President?* In Volume II of the Report, Mueller states that "The President's efforts to influence the investigation were mostly unsuccessful, but that is largely because the persons who surrounded the President declined to carry out orders or accede to his requests. Comey did not end the investigation of Flynn, which ultimately resulted in Flynn's prosecution and conviction for lying to the FBI. McGahn did not tell the Acting Attorney General that the Special Counsel must be removed, but was instead prepared to resign over the President's order. Lewandowski and Dearborn did not deliver the President's message to Sessions that he should confine the Russia investigation to future election meddling only. And McGahn refused to recede from his recollections about events surrounding the President's direction to have the Special Counsel removed, despite the President's multiple demands that he do so." To what extent should the fact that President's aides refused to help him hinder the investigation matter in deciding whether to impeach?

4. *What should the House do?* If you were a member of the House of Representatives, would you vote for impeachment based on either Volume I or Volume II of the Mueller Report? Why or why not? To what extent should the following considerations be relevant to your decision:

a. The President's popularity.

b. The views of your constituents about impeachment.

c. The views of the national public about impeachment.

d. The likelihood that the Senate will or will not convict.

e. The number of months before the upcoming 2020 elections, which will decide whether the President gets a second term or is voted out of office.

Are elections a good substitute for impeachment? If the House does nothing and the President loses, does that mean impeachment was a bad idea? If the House does nothing and the President wins a second term, does *that* mean that impeachment was a bad idea?

Should members of the House refuse to impeach if they do not want the President to win a second term and fear that impeachment and acquittal in the Senate will help the President win reelection? If the House is akin to a prosecutor, to what extent is this a legitimate consideration?

76. Amber Phillips, Mueller's statement, annotated: 'If we had had confidence that the president clearly did not commit a crime, we would have said so', Washington Post, May 29, 2019, https://www. washingtonpost.com/politics/2019/05/29/muellers-statement-annotated-if-we-had-confidence-that-president-clearly-did-not-commit-crime-we-would-have-said-so/?utm_term=.ef48027f00a4

Chapter 7

Race and the Equal Protection Clause

Insert at the end of p. 1247:

TRUMP v. HAWAII
138 S. Ct. 2392 (2018)

[During the 2016 Presidential campaign, Donald Trump ran on a platform of restricting illegal immigration, deporting undocumented aliens, and preventing the United States from being invaded by radical Islamists. He strongly opposed receiving refugees from Syria fleeing that country's civil war. On December 7, 2015, following a mass shooting in San Bernadino, California, candidate Trump gave a speech in which he called for "a total and complete shutdown of Muslims entering the United States until our country's representatives can figure out what is going on." The proposal for what became known as a "Muslim ban" was posted on Trump's campaign website until March 2017. During the 2016 campaign Trump and his surrogates alternatively described the proposal as a ban on people coming from countries known to produce terrorism, along with a call for "extreme vetting" of people entering the United States.

Shortly after taking office, President Trump signed Executive Order No. 13769, Protecting the Nation From Foreign Terrorist Entry Into the United States. 82 Fed.Reg. 8977 (2017) (EO-1). EO-1 directed the Secretary of Homeland Security to conduct a review to examine the adequacy of information provided by foreign governments about their nationals seeking to enter the United States. Pending that review, the order suspended for 90 days the entry of foreign nationals from seven countries—Iran, Iraq, Libya, Somalia, Sudan, Syria, and Yemen—that had been previously identified by Congress or prior administrations as posing heightened terrorism risks. EO-1 also modified refugee policy. It suspended the United States Refugee Admissions Program (USRAP) for 120 days and reduced the number of refugees eligible to be admitted to the United States during fiscal year 2017 from 110,000 to 50,000. The refugee provisions were not at issue in the litigation before the Supreme Court.

EO-1 created enormous confusion at airports around the United States, in part because it was not immediately clear—even to federal officials—whether the order applied to permanent residents of the United States (green card holders) who were also nationals of the seven countries. On January 28, protests against the order began around the country and at various airports. A week after

EO-1 was issued, a Federal District Court in Washington state entered a nation-wide temporary restraining order enjoining enforcement of several of its key provisions. Six days later, the Ninth Circuit denied the Government's emergency motion to stay the order pending appeal. Washington v. Trump, 847 F.3d 1151 (2017) (*per curiam*).

In response, the President revoked EO-1, replacing it with Executive Order No. 13780 (EO-2), which again directed a worldwide review. EO-2 also temporarily restricted the entry (with case-by-case waivers) of foreign nationals from six of the countries covered by EO-1: Iran, Libya, Somalia, Sudan, Syria, and Yemen, eliminating Iraq. The order explained that those countries had been selected because each "is a state sponsor of terrorism, has been significantly compromised by terrorist organizations, or contains active conflict zones." The entry restriction was to stay in effect for 90 days, pending completion of the worldwide review.

EO-2 was immediately challenged in court, and district courts in Maryland and Hawaii issued nationwide preliminary injunctions barring enforcement of the entry suspension; the Fourth and Ninth circuits affirmed. The Supreme Court granted certiorari, staying the injunctions—allowing the entry suspension to go into effect—with respect to foreign nationals who lacked a "credible claim of a bona fide relationship" with a person or entity in the United States. However, the temporary restrictions in EO-2 expired before a decision on the merits, and so the Supreme Court vacated the lower court decisions as moot.

Shortly thereafter, President Trump issued a third executive order, Proclamation No. 9645, Enhancing Vetting Capabilities and Processes for Detecting Attempted Entry Into the United States by Terrorists or Other Public–Safety Threats, which was immediately challenged in court.

Plaintiffs—the State of Hawaii, three individuals with foreign relatives affected by the entry suspension, and the Muslim Association of Hawaii—argued that the Proclamation violated the Immigration and Nationality Act (INA) and the Establishment Clause.]

Chief Justice ROBERTS delivered the opinion of the Court.

I

The Proclamation (as its title indicates) sought to improve vetting procedures [for foreign nationals traveling to the United States] by identifying ongoing deficiencies in the information needed to assess whether nationals of particular countries present "public safety threats." § 1(a). To further that purpose, the Proclamation placed entry restrictions on the nationals of eight foreign states whose systems for managing and sharing information about their nationals the President deemed inadequate.

The Proclamation described how foreign states were selected for inclusion based on the review undertaken pursuant to EO-2. [T]he Department of Homeland Security (DHS), in consultation with the State Department and several intelligence agencies, developed [an informational and risk assessment] "baseline" for . . . foreign governments. . . . DHS collected and evaluated data regarding all foreign governments [identifying] countries [that had or risked] having deficient information-sharing practices and [that] present[ed] national security concerns. The State Department then undertook diplomatic efforts over a 50–day period to encourage all foreign governments to improve their practices.

Following the 50–day period, the Acting Secretary of Homeland Security concluded that eight countries—Chad, Iran, Iraq, Libya, North Korea, Syria, Venezuela, and Yemen—remained deficient in terms of their risk profile and willingness to provide requested information. The Acting Secretary recommended that the President impose entry restrictions on certain nationals from all of those countries except Iraq [because the United States was working with Iraq to combat ISIS]. She also [recommended including] Somalia [because it had a] "significant terrorist presence."

After consulting with multiple Cabinet members and other officials, the President adopted the Acting Secretary's recommendations and issued the Proclamation. Invoking his authority under 8 U.S.C. §§ 1182(f) and 1185(a), the President determined that certain entry restrictions were necessary to "prevent the entry of those foreign nationals about whom the United States Government lacks sufficient information"; "elicit improved identity management and information-sharing protocols and practices from foreign governments"; and otherwise "advance [the] foreign policy, national security, and counterterrorism objectives" of the United States. . . .

The Proclamation imposed a range of restrictions that vary based on the "distinct circumstances" in each of the eight countries. . . . [It] exempts lawful permanent residents and foreign nationals who have been granted asylum. It also provides for case-by-case waivers when a foreign national demonstrates undue hardship, and that his entry is in the national interest and would not pose a threat to public safety. § 3(c)(i); see also § 3(c)(iv) (listing examples of when a waiver might be appropriate, such as if the foreign national seeks to reside with a close family member, obtain urgent medical care, or pursue significant business obligations). The Proclamation further directs DHS to assess on a continuing basis whether entry restrictions should be modified or continued, and to report to the President every 180 days. Upon completion of the first such review period, the President, on the recommendation of the Secretary of Homeland Security, determined that Chad had sufficiently improved its practices, and he accordingly lifted restrictions on its nationals. . . .

III

. . . Congress has . . . delegated to the President authority to suspend or restrict the entry of aliens in certain circumstances. The principal source of that authority, . . . § 1182(f), states: "Whenever the President finds that the entry of any aliens or of any class of aliens into the United States would be detrimental to the interests of the United States, he may by proclamation, and for such period as he shall deem necessary, suspend the entry of all aliens or any class of aliens as immigrants or nonimmigrants, or impose on the entry of aliens any restrictions he may deem to be appropriate."

By its terms, § 1182(f) exudes deference to the President in every clause. It entrusts to the President the decisions whether and when to suspend entry

. . .; whose entry to suspend . . .; for how long . . .; and on what conditions. . . . The Proclamation falls well within this comprehensive delegation. The sole prerequisite set forth in § 1182(f) is that the President "find[ ]" that the entry of the covered aliens "would be detrimental to the interests of the United States." The President has undoubtedly fulfilled that requirement here. He first ordered DHS and other agencies to conduct a comprehensive evaluation of every single country's compliance with the information and risk assessment baseline. The President then issued a Proclamation setting forth extensive findings describing how deficiencies in the practices of select foreign governments — several of which are state sponsors of terrorism — deprive the Government of "sufficient information to assess the risks [those countries' nationals] pose to the United States." Based on that review, the President found that it was in the national interest to restrict entry of aliens who could not be vetted with adequate information — both to protect national security and public safety, and to induce improvement by their home countries. . . .

Plaintiffs . . . argue . . . that the Proclamation fails to provide a persuasive rationale for why nationality alone renders the covered foreign nationals a security risk. And they further discount the President's stated concern about deficient vetting because the Proclamation allows many aliens from the designated countries to enter on nonimmigrant visas.

Such arguments [assume] that § 1182(f) not only requires the President to *make* a finding that entry "would be detrimental to the interests of the United States," but also to explain that finding with sufficient detail to enable judicial review. That premise is questionable. But even assuming that some form of review is appropriate, plaintiffs' attacks on the sufficiency of the President's findings cannot be sustained. The 12–page Proclamation — which thoroughly describes the process, agency evaluations, and recommendations underlying the President's chosen restrictions — is more detailed than any prior order a President has issued under § 1182(f). Moreover, plaintiffs' request for a searching inquiry into the persuasiveness of the President's justifications is inconsistent with the broad statutory text and the deference traditionally accorded the President in this sphere. "Whether the President's chosen method" of addressing perceived risks is justified from a policy perspective is "irrelevant to the scope of his [§ 1182(f)] authority." *Sale v. Haitian Centers Council, Inc.,* 509 U.S. 155, 187-188 (1993). And when the President adopts "a preventive measure . . . in the context of international affairs and national security," he is "not required to conclusively link all of the pieces in the puzzle before [courts] grant weight to [his] empirical conclusions." *Holder v. Humanitarian Law Project,* 561 U.S. 1, 35 (2010).

The Proclamation also comports with the remaining textual limits in § 1182(f). We agree with plaintiffs that the word "suspend" often connotes a "defer[ral] till later." But that does not mean that the President is required to prescribe in advance a fixed end date for the entry restrictions. . . . Like its predecessors, the Proclamation makes clear that its "conditional restrictions" will remain in force only so long as necessary to "address" the identified "inadequacies and risks" within the covered nations. To that end, the Proclamation establishes an ongoing process to engage covered nations and assess every 180 days whether the entry restrictions should be modified or terminated. Indeed, after the initial review period, the President determined that Chad had made sufficient improvements to its identity-management protocols, and he accordingly lifted the entry suspension on its nationals.

. . . We may assume that § 1182(f) does not allow the President to expressly override particular provisions of the INA. But plaintiffs have not identified any conflict between the statute and the Proclamation that would implicitly bar the President from addressing deficiencies in the Nation's vetting system.

To the contrary, the Proclamation supports Congress's individualized approach for determining admissibility. The INA sets forth various inadmissibility grounds based on connections to terrorism and criminal history, but those provisions can only work when the consular officer has sufficient (and sufficiently reliable) information to make that determination. The Proclamation promotes the effectiveness of the vetting process by helping to ensure the availability of such information. . . . Nor is there a conflict between the Proclamation and the Visa Waiver Program [which] allows travel without a visa for short-term visitors from 38 countries that have entered into a "rigorous security partnership" with the United States. Congress's decision to authorize a benefit for "many of America's closest allies," did not implicitly foreclose the Executive from imposing tighter restrictions on nationals of certain high-risk countries. . . . Fairly read, [§ 1182(f)] vests authority in the President to impose additional limitations on entry beyond the grounds for exclusion set forth in the INA—including in response to circumstances that might affect the vetting system or other "interests of the United States." . . . [Moreover,] Presidents have repeatedly suspended entry not because the covered nationals themselves engaged in harmful acts but instead to retaliate for conduct by their governments that conflicted with U.S. foreign policy interests. . . .

Plaintiffs' final statutory argument is that the President's entry suspension violates § 1152(a)(1)(A), which provides that "no person shall . . . be discriminated against in the issuance of an immigrant visa because of the person's race, sex, nationality, place of birth, or place of residence." . . . [T]his argument challenges only the validity of the entry restrictions on *immigrant* travel. . . . [P]laintiffs' reading would not affect any of the limitations on nonimmigrant travel in the Proclamation.

In any event, we reject plaintiffs' interpretation because it ignores the basic distinction between admissibility determinations and visa issuance that runs throughout the INA. Section 1182 defines the pool of individuals who are admissible to the United States. [For example,] any alien who is inadmissible under § 1182 (based on, for example, health risks, criminal history, or foreign policy consequences) is screened out as "ineligible to receive a visa." . . . Once § 1182 sets the boundaries of admissibility into the United States, § 1152(a)(1)(A) prohibits discrimination in the allocation of immigrant visas based on nationality and other traits. . . . Had Congress instead intended in § 1152(a)(1)(A) to constrain the President's power to determine who may enter the country, it could easily have chosen language directed to that end. . . . Common sense and historical practice confirm [that] [§]1152(a)(1)(A) has never been treated as a constraint on the criteria for admissibility in § 1182. Presidents have repeatedly exercised their authority to suspend entry on the basis of nationality. . . . President Reagan relied on § 1182(f) to suspend entry "as immigrants by all Cuban nationals," subject to exceptions. Likewise, President Carter invoked § 1185(a)(1) to deny and revoke visas to all Iranian nationals.

On plaintiffs' reading, those orders were beyond the President's authority. The entry restrictions in the Proclamation on North Korea (which plaintiffs do not challenge in this litigation) would also be unlawful. Nor would the President be permitted to suspend entry from particular foreign states in response to an epidemic confined to a single region, or a verified terrorist threat involving nationals of a specific foreign nation, or even if the United States were on the brink of war. . . .

IV

We now turn to plaintiffs' claim that the Proclamation was issued for the unconstitutional purpose of excluding Muslims. . . . [T]he individual plaintiffs have Article III standing to challenge the exclusion of their relatives under the Establishment Clause.

[O]ur cases recognize that "[t]he clearest command of the Establishment Clause is that one religious denomination cannot be officially preferred over another." *Larson v. Valente,* 456 U.S. 228, 244 (1982). Plaintiffs believe that the Proclamation violates this prohibition by singling out Muslims for disfavored treatment. The entry suspension, they contend, operates as a "religious gerrymander," in part because most of the countries covered by the Proclamation have Muslim-majority populations. . . . [P]laintiffs allege that the primary purpose of the Proclamation was religious animus and that the President's stated concerns about vetting protocols and national security were but pretexts for discriminating against Muslims.

At the heart of plaintiffs' case is a series of statements by the President and his advisers casting doubt on the official objective of the Proclamation. For example, while a candidate on the campaign trail, the President published a "Statement on Preventing Muslim Immigration" that called for a "total and complete shutdown of Muslims entering the United States until our country's representatives can figure out what is going on." That statement remained on his campaign website until May 2017. Then-candidate Trump also stated that "Islam hates us" and asserted that the United States was "having problems with Muslims coming into the country." Shortly after being elected, when asked whether violence in Europe had affected his plans to "ban Muslim immigration," the President replied, "You know my plans. All along, I've been proven to be right."

One week after his inauguration, the President issued EO-1. In a television interview, one of the President's campaign advisers explained that when the President "first announced it, he said, 'Muslim ban.' He called me up. He said, 'Put a commission together. Show me the right way to do it legally.'" The adviser said he assembled a group of Members of Congress and lawyers that "focused on, instead of religion, danger. . . . [The order] is based on places where there [is] substantial evidence that people are sending terrorists into our country."

Plaintiffs also note that after issuing EO–2 to replace EO–1, the President expressed regret that his prior order had been "watered down" and called for a "much tougher version" of his "Travel Ban." Shortly before the release of the Proclamation, he stated that the "travel ban . . . should be far larger, tougher, and more specific," but "stupidly that would not be politically correct." More recently, on November 29, 2017, the President retweeted links to three anti-Muslim propaganda videos. In response to questions about those videos, the President's deputy press secretary denied that the President thinks Muslims are a threat to the United States, explaining that "the President has been talking about these security issues for years now, from the campaign trail to the White House" and "has addressed these issues with the travel order that he issued earlier this year and the companion proclamation."

The President of the United States possesses an extraordinary power to speak to his fellow citizens and on their behalf. Our Presidents have frequently used that power to espouse the principles of religious freedom and tolerance on which this Nation was founded. In 1790 George Washington reassured the Hebrew Congregation of Newport, Rhode Island that "happily the Government of the United States . . . gives to bigotry no sanction, to persecution no assistance [and] requires only that they who live under its protection should demean themselves as good citizens." President Eisenhower, at the opening of the Islamic Center of Washington, similarly pledged to a Muslim audience that "America would fight with her whole strength for your right to have here your own church," declaring that "[t]his concept is indeed a part of America." And just days after the attacks of September 11, 2001, President George W. Bush returned to the same Islamic Center to implore his fellow Americans—Muslims and non-Muslims alike—to remember during their time of grief that "[t]he face of terror is not the true faith of Islam," and that America is "a great country because we share the same values of respect and dignity and human worth." Yet it cannot be denied that the Federal Government and the Presidents who have carried its laws into effect have—from the Nation's earliest days—performed unevenly in living up to those inspiring words.

Plaintiffs argue that this President's words strike at fundamental standards of respect and tolerance, in violation of our constitutional tradition. But the issue before us is not whether to denounce the statements. It is instead the significance of those statements in reviewing a Presidential directive, neutral on its face, addressing a matter within the core of executive responsibility. In doing so, we must consider not only the statements of a particular President, but also the authority of the Presidency itself.

The case before us differs in numerous respects from the conventional Establishment Clause claim. Unlike the typical suit involving religious displays or school prayer, plaintiffs seek to invalidate a national security directive regulating the entry of aliens abroad. Their claim accordingly raises a number of delicate issues regarding the scope of the constitutional right and the manner of proof. The Proclamation, moreover, is facially neutral toward religion. Plaintiffs therefore ask the Court to probe the sincerity of the stated justifications for the policy by reference to extrinsic statements—many of which were made before the President took the oath of office. These various aspects of plaintiffs' challenge inform our standard of review.

For more than a century, this Court has recognized that the admission and exclusion of foreign nationals is a "fundamental sovereign attribute exercised by the Government's political departments largely immune from judicial control." *Fiallo v. Bell,* 430 U.S. 787 (1977); see *Harisiades v. Shaughnessy,* 342 U.S. 580, 588–589 (1952) ("[A]ny policy toward aliens is vitally and intricately interwoven with contemporaneous policies in regard to the conduct of foreign relations [and] the war power."). Because decisions in these matters may implicate "relations with foreign powers," or involve "classifications defined in the light of changing political and economic circumstances," such judgments "are frequently of a character more appropriate to either the Legislature or the Executive." *Mathews v. Diaz,* 426 U.S. 67, 81 (1976).

Nonetheless, although foreign nationals seeking admission have no constitutional right to entry, this Court has engaged in a circumscribed judicial inquiry when the denial of a visa allegedly burdens the constitutional rights of a U.S. citizen. In *Kleindienst v. Mandel,* 408 U.S. 753 (1972), the Attorney General denied admission to a Belgian journalist and self-described "revolutionary Marxist," Ernest Mandel, who had been invited to speak at a conference at Stanford University. The professors who wished to hear Mandel speak challenged that decision under the First Amendment, and we acknowledged that their constitutional "right to receive information" was implicated. But we limited our review to whether the Executive gave a "facially legitimate and bona fide" reason for its action. Given the authority of the political branches over admission, we held that "when the Executive exercises this [delegated] power negatively on the basis of a facially legitimate and bona fide reason, the courts will neither look behind the exercise of that discretion, nor test it by balancing its justification" against the asserted constitutional interests of U.S. citizens.

The principal dissent [by Justice Sotomayor] suggests that *Mandel* has no bearing on this case, but our opinions have reaffirmed and applied its deferential standard of review across different contexts and constitutional claims. In *Din,* JUSTICE KENNEDY reiterated that "respect for the political branches' broad power over the creation and administration of the immigration system" meant that the Government need provide only a statutory citation to explain a visa denial. Likewise in *Fiallo,* we applied *Mandel* to a "broad congressional policy" giving immigration preferences to mothers of illegitimate children. Even though the statute created a "categorical" entry classification that discriminated on the basis of sex and legitimacy, the Court concluded that "it is not the judicial role in cases of this sort to probe and test the justifications" of immigration policies. . . .

Mandel's narrow standard of review "has particular force" in admission and immigration cases that overlap with "the area of national security." For one, "[j]udicial inquiry into the national-security realm raises concerns for the separation of powers" by intruding on the President's constitutional responsibilities in the area of foreign affairs. *Ziglar v. Abbasi,* 582 U.S. ____ (2017). For another, "when it comes to collecting evidence and drawing inferences" on questions of national security, "the lack of competence on the part of the courts is marked." *Humanitarian Law Project.*

The upshot of our cases in this context is clear: "Any rule of constitutional law that would inhibit the flexibility" of the President "to respond to changing world conditions should be adopted only with the greatest caution," and our inquiry into matters of entry and national security is highly constrained. *Mathews.* We need not define the precise contours of that inquiry in this case. A conventional application of *Mandel,* asking only whether the policy is facially legitimate and bona fide, would put an end to our review. But the Government has suggested that it may be appropriate here for the inquiry to extend beyond the facial neutrality of the order. For our purposes today, we assume that we may look behind the face of the Proclamation to the extent of applying rational basis review. That standard of review considers whether the entry policy is plausibly related to the Government's stated objective to protect the country and improve vetting processes. See *Railroad Retirement Bd. v. Fritz,* 449 U.S. 166, 179 (1980). As a result, we may consider plaintiffs' extrinsic evidence, but will uphold the policy so long as it can reasonably be understood to result from a justification independent of unconstitutional grounds.

The dissent finds "perplexing" the application of rational basis review in this context. But what is far more problematic is the dissent's assumption that courts should review immigration policies, diplomatic sanctions, and military actions under the *de novo* "reasonable observer" inquiry applicable to cases involving holiday displays and graduation ceremonies. [A] circumscribed inquiry applies to any constitutional claim concerning the entry of foreign nationals. The dissent can cite no authority for its proposition that the more free-ranging inquiry it proposes is appropriate in the national security and foreign affairs context. [relocated footnote—eds.]

Given the standard of review, it should come as no surprise that the Court hardly ever strikes down a policy as illegitimate under rational basis scrutiny. On the few occasions where we have done so, a common thread has been that the laws at issue lack any purpose other than a "bare . . . desire to harm a politically unpopular group." *Department of Agriculture v. Moreno,* 413 U.S. 528, 534 (1973). In one case, we invalidated a local zoning ordinance that required a special permit for group homes for the intellectually disabled, but not for other facilities such as fraternity houses or hospitals. We did so on the ground that the city's stated concerns about (among other things) "legal responsibility" and "crowded conditions" rested on "an irrational prejudice" against the intellectually disabled. *Cleburne v. Cleburne Living Center, Inc.,* 473 U.S. 432, 448–450 (1985). And in another case, this Court overturned a state constitutional amendment that denied gays and lesbians access to the protection of antidiscrimination laws. The amendment, we held, was "divorced from any factual context from which we could discern a relationship to legitimate state interests," and "its sheer breadth [was] so discontinuous with the reasons offered for it" that the initiative seemed "inexplicable by anything but animus." *Romer v. Evans,* 517 U.S. 620, 632, 635 (1996).

The Proclamation does not fit this pattern. It cannot be said that it is impossible to "discern a relationship to legitimate state interests" or that the policy is "inexplicable by anything but animus." Indeed, the dissent can only attempt to argue otherwise by refusing to apply anything resembling rational basis review. But because there is persuasive evidence that the entry suspension has a legitimate grounding in national security concerns, quite apart from any religious hostility, we must accept that independent justification.

The Proclamation is expressly premised on legitimate purposes: preventing entry of nationals who cannot be adequately vetted and inducing other nations to improve their practices. The text says nothing about religion. Plaintiffs and the dissent nonetheless emphasize that five of the seven nations currently included in the Proclamation have Muslim-majority populations. Yet that fact alone does not support an inference of religious hostility, given that the policy covers just 8% of the world's Muslim population and is limited to countries that were previously designated by Congress or prior administrations as posing national security risks.

The Proclamation, moreover, reflects the results of a worldwide review process undertaken by multiple Cabinet officials and their agencies. Plaintiffs seek to discredit the findings of the review, pointing to deviations from the review's baseline criteria resulting in the inclusion of Somalia and omission of Iraq. But as the Proclamation explains, in each case the determinations were justified by the distinct conditions in each country. . . . The dissent likewise doubts the thoroughness of the multi-agency review because a recent Freedom of Information Act request shows that the final DHS report "was a mere 17 pages." Yet a simple page count offers little insight into the actual substance of the final report, much less pre-decisional materials underlying it.

More fundamentally, plaintiffs and the dissent challenge the entry suspension based on their perception of its effectiveness and wisdom. They suggest that the policy is overbroad and does little to serve national security interests. But we cannot substitute our own assessment for the Executive's predictive judgments on such matters, all of which "are delicate, complex, and involve large elements of prophecy." While we of course "do not defer to the Government's reading of the First Amendment," the Executive's evaluation of the underlying facts is entitled to appropriate weight, particularly in the context of litigation involving "sensitive and weighty interests of national security and foreign affairs." *Humanitarian Law Project.*

Three additional features of the entry policy support the Government's claim of a legitimate national security interest. First, since the President introduced entry restrictions in January 2017, three Muslim-majority countries—Iraq, Sudan, and Chad—have been removed from the list of covered countries. . . . Second, for those countries that remain subject to entry restrictions, the Proclamation includes significant exceptions for various categories of foreign nationals. The policy permits nationals from nearly every covered country to travel to the United States on a variety of nonimmigrant visas. . . . These carveouts for nonimmigrant visas are substantial: Over the last three fiscal years—before the Proclamation was in effect—the majority of visas issued to nationals from the covered countries were nonimmigrant visas. The Proclamation also exempts permanent residents and individuals who have been granted asylum. Third, the Proclamation creates a waiver program open to all covered foreign nationals seeking entry as immigrants or nonimmigrants. According to the Proclamation, consular officers are to consider in each admissibility determination whether the alien demonstrates that (1) denying entry would cause undue hardship; (2) entry would not pose a threat to public safety; and (3) entry would be in the interest of the United States. . . .

Finally, the dissent invokes *Korematsu v. United States,* 323 U.S. 214 (1944). Whatever rhetorical advantage the dissent may see in doing so, *Korematsu* has nothing to do with this case. The forcible relocation of U.S. citizens to concentration camps, solely and explicitly on the basis of race, is objectively unlawful and outside the scope of Presidential authority. But it is wholly inapt to liken that morally repugnant order to a facially neutral policy denying certain foreign nationals the privilege of admission. The entry suspension is an act that is well within executive authority and could have been taken by any other President — the only question is evaluating the actions of this particular President in promulgating an otherwise valid Proclamation.

The dissent's reference to *Korematsu,* however, affords this Court the opportunity to make express what is already obvious: *Korematsu* was gravely wrong the day it was decided, has been overruled in the court of history, and — to be clear — "has no place in law under the Constitution."

Under these circumstances, the Government has set forth a sufficient national security justification to survive rational basis review. We express no view on the soundness of the policy. We simply hold today that plaintiffs have not demonstrated a likelihood of success on the merits of their constitutional claim.

V

Because plaintiffs have not shown that they are likely to succeed on the merits of their claims, we reverse the grant of the preliminary injunction as an abuse of discretion. The case now returns to the lower courts for such further proceedings as may be appropriate. Our disposition of the case makes it unnecessary to consider the propriety of the nationwide scope of the injunction issued by the District Court.

The judgment of the Court of Appeals is reversed, and the case is remanded for further proceedings consistent with this opinion.

It is so ordered.

JUSTICE KENNEDY, concurring.

I join the Court's opinion in full.

There may be some common ground between the opinions in this case, in that the Court does acknowledge that in some instances, governmental action may be subject to judicial review to determine whether or not it is "inexplicable by anything but animus," *Romer v. Evans,* which in this case would be animosity to a religion. Whether judicial proceedings may properly continue in this case, in light of the substantial deference that is and must be accorded to the Executive in the conduct of foreign affairs, and in light of today's decision, is a matter to be addressed in the first instance on remand. And even if further proceedings are permitted, it would be necessary to determine that any discovery and other preliminary matters would not themselves intrude on the foreign affairs power of the Executive.

In all events, it is appropriate to make this further observation. There are numerous instances in which the statements and actions of Government officials are not subject to judicial scrutiny or intervention. That does not mean those officials are free to disregard the Constitution and the rights it proclaims and protects. The oath that all officials take to adhere to the Constitution is not confined to those spheres in which the Judiciary can correct or even comment upon what those officials say or do. Indeed, the very fact that an official may have broad discretion, discretion free from judicial scrutiny, makes it all the more imperative for him or her to adhere to the Constitution and to its meaning and its promise.

The First Amendment prohibits the establishment of religion and promises the free exercise of religion. From these safeguards, and from the guarantee of freedom of speech, it follows there is freedom of belief and expression. It is an urgent necessity that officials adhere to these constitutional guarantees and mandates in all their actions, even in the sphere of foreign affairs. An anxious world must know that our Government remains committed always to the liberties the Constitution seeks to preserve and protect, so that freedom extends outward, and lasts.

[Justice Thomas concurred, arguing that he was "skeptical that district courts have the authority to enter universal injunctions" covering the entire nation.]

[Justice Breyer, joined by Justice Kagan, dissented. He argued that there was evidence that the government was not serious about providing case-by-case waivers to provide visas for people — including especially Muslims — who had strong reasons for a visa and who posed no security threats. Such people included, among others, lawful permanent residents, asylum seekers, refugees, students, and children. Because the waiver requirement appeared to be a sham, it raised an inference that the Proclamation was motivated by animus toward Muslims rather than genuine security needs. Accordingly, Justice Breyer argued for a remand to the lower courts for further fact finding. "If this Court must decide the question without this further litigation, I would, on balance, find the evidence of antireligious bias . . . a sufficient basis to set the Proclamation aside."]

JUSTICE SOTOMAYOR, with whom JUSTICE GINSBURG joins, dissenting.

The United States of America is a Nation built upon the promise of religious liberty. Our Founders honored that core promise by embedding the principle of religious neutrality in the First Amendment. The Court's decision today fails to safeguard that fundamental principle. It leaves undisturbed a policy first advertised openly and unequivocally as a "total and complete shutdown of Muslims entering the United States" because the policy now masquerades behind a facade of national-security concerns. But this repackaging does little to cleanse Presidential Proclamation No. 9645 of the appearance of discrimination that the President's words have created. Based on the evidence in the record, a reasonable observer would conclude that the Proclamation was motivated by anti-Muslim animus. That alone suffices to show that plaintiffs are likely to succeed on the merits of their Establishment Clause claim. The majority holds otherwise by ignoring the facts, misconstruing our legal precedent, and turning a blind eye to the pain and suffering the Proclamation inflicts upon countless families and individuals, many of whom are United States citizens. Because that troubling result runs contrary to the Constitution and our precedent, I dissent.

I

[T]he "clearest command" of the Establishment Clause is that the Government cannot favor or disfavor one religion over another. *Larson v. Valente,* 456 U.S. 228, 244 (1982). . . . "When the government acts with the ostensible and predominant purpose" of disfavoring a particular religion, "it violates that central Establishment Clause value of official religious neutrality, there being no neutrality when the government's ostensible object is to take sides." *McCreary County v. American Civil Liberties Union of Ky.,* 545 U.S. 844, 860 (2005). To determine whether plaintiffs have proved an Establishment Clause violation, the Court asks whether a reasonable observer would view the government action as enacted for the purpose of disfavoring a religion.

In answering that question, this Court has generally considered the text of the government policy, its operation, and any available evidence regarding "the historical background of the decision under challenge, the specific series of events leading to the enactment or official policy in question, and the legislative or administrative history, including contemporaneous statements made by" the decisionmaker. At the same time, however, courts must take care not to engage in "any judicial psychoanalysis of a drafter's heart of hearts."

Although the majority briefly recounts a few of the statements and background events that form the basis of plaintiffs' constitutional challenge, *ante,* at 27–28, that highly abridged account does not tell even half of the story. The full record paints a far more harrowing picture, from which a reasonable observer would readily conclude that the Proclamation was motivated by hostility and animus toward the Muslim faith.

During his Presidential campaign, then-candidate Donald Trump pledged that, if elected, he would ban Muslims from entering the United States. Specifically, on December 7, 2015, he issued a formal statement "calling for a total and complete shutdown of Muslims entering the United States." That statement, which remained on his campaign website until May 2017 (several months into his Presidency), read in full:

> "Donald J. Trump is calling for a total and complete shutdown of Muslims entering the United States until our country's representatives can figure out what is going on. According to Pew Research, among others, there is great hatred towards Americans by large segments of the Muslim population. Most recently, a poll from the Center for Security Policy released data showing '25% of those polled agreed that violence against Americans here in the United States is justified as a part of

the global jihad' and 51% of those polled 'agreed that Muslims in America should
have the choice of being governed according to Shariah.' Shariah authorizes such
atrocities as murder against nonbelievers who won't convert, beheadings and more
unthinkable acts that pose great harm to Americans, especially women.

"Mr. Trum[p] stated, 'Without looking at the various polling data, it is obvious
to anybody the hatred is beyond comprehension. Where this hatred comes from
and why we will have to determine. Until we are able to determine and understand
this problem and the dangerous threat it poses, our country cannot be the victims
of the horrendous attacks by people that believe only in Jihad, and have no sense of
reason or respect of human life. If I win the election for President, we are going to
Make America Great Again.' —Donald J. Trump."

On December 8, 2015, Trump justified his proposal during a television
interview by noting that President Franklin D. Roosevelt "did the same thing"
with respect to the internment of Japanese Americans during World War II. In
January 2016, during a Republican primary debate, Trump was asked whether
he wanted to "rethink [his] position" on "banning Muslims from entering the
country." He answered, "No." A month later, at a rally in South Carolina, Trump
told an apocryphal story about United States General John J. Pershing killing a
large group of Muslim insurgents in the Philippines with bullets dipped in pigs'
blood in the early 1900's. In March 2016, he expressed his belief that "Islam
hates us. . . . [W]e can't allow people coming into this country who have this
hatred of the United States . . . [a]nd of people that are not Muslim." That same
month, Trump asserted that "[w]e're having problems with the Muslims, and
we're having problems with Muslims coming into the country." He therefore
called for surveillance of mosques in the United States, blaming terrorist attacks
on Muslims' lack of "assimilation" and their commitment to "sharia law." A day
later, he opined that Muslims "do not respect us at all" and "don't respect a lot
of the things that are happening throughout not only our country, but they don't
respect other things."

As Trump's presidential campaign progressed, he began to describe his policy
proposal in slightly different terms. In June 2016, for instance, he character-
ized the policy proposal as a suspension of immigration from countries "where
there's a proven history of terrorism." He also described the proposal as rooted
in the need to stop "importing radical Islamic terrorism to the West through a
failed immigration system." Asked in July 2016 whether he was "pull[ing] back
from" his pledged Muslim ban, Trump responded, "I actually don't think it's a
rollback. In fact, you could say it's an expansion." He then explained that he
used different terminology because "[p]eople were so upset when [he] used the
word Muslim."

A month before the 2016 election, Trump reiterated that his proposed "Muslim
ban" had "morphed into a[n] extreme vetting from certain areas of the world."
Then, on December 21, 2016, President-elect Trump was asked whether he
would "rethink" his previous "plans to create a Muslim registry or ban Muslim
immigration." He replied: "You know my plans. All along, I've proven to be
right."

On January 27, 2017, one week after taking office, President Trump signed Executive Order No. 13769, 82 Fed. Reg. 8977 (2017) (EO-1), entitled "Protecting the Nation From Foreign Terrorist Entry Into the United States." As he signed it, President Trump read the title, looked up, and said "We all know what that means." That same day, President Trump explained to the media that, under EO-1, Christians would be given priority for entry as refugees into the United States. In particular, he bemoaned the fact that in the past, "[i]f you were a Muslim [refugee from Syria] you could come in, but if you were a Christian, it was almost impossible." Considering that past policy "very unfair," President Trump explained that EO-1 was designed "to help" the Christians in Syria. The following day, one of President Trump's key advisers candidly drew the connection between EO-1 and the "Muslim ban" that the President had pledged to implement if elected. According to that adviser, "[W]hen [Donald Trump] first announced it, he said, 'Muslim ban.' He called me up. He said, 'Put a commission together. Show me the right way to do it legally.'"

[After the 9th Circuit upheld a district court's injunction of EO-1], the Government declined to continue defending EO–1 in court and instead announced that the President intended to issue a new executive order. . . . One of the President's senior advisers publicly explained that EO-2 would "have the same basic policy outcome" as EO-1, and that any changes would address "very technical issues that were brought up by the court." After EO-2 was issued, the White House Press Secretary told reporters that, by issuing EO-2, President Trump "continue[d] to deliver on . . . his most significant campaign promises." That statement was consistent with President Trump's own declaration that "I keep my campaign promises, and our citizens will be very happy when they see the result." . . .

While litigation over EO-2 was ongoing, President Trump repeatedly made statements alluding to a desire to keep Muslims out of the country. For instance, he said at a rally of his supporters that EO-2 was just a "watered down version of the first one" and had been "tailor[ed]" at the behest of "the lawyers." He further added that he would prefer "to go back to the first [executive order] and go all the way" and reiterated his belief that it was "very hard" for Muslims to assimilate into Western culture. During a rally in April 2017, President Trump recited the lyrics to a song called "The Snake," a song about a woman who nurses a sick snake back to health but then is attacked by the snake, as a warning about Syrian refugees entering the country. And in June 2017, the President stated on Twitter that the Justice Department had submitted a "watered down, politically correct version" of the "original Travel Ban" "to S[upreme] C[ourt]."

According to the White House, President Trump's statements on Twitter are "official statements." [relocated footnote—eds.]

The President went on to tweet: "People, the lawyers and the courts can call it whatever they want, but I am calling it what we need and what it is, a TRAVEL BAN!" He added: "That's right, we need a TRAVEL BAN for certain DANGEROUS countries, not some politically correct term that won't help us protect our people!" Then, on August 17, 2017, President Trump issued yet another tweet about Islam, once more referencing the story about General Pershing's massacre of Muslims in the Philippines: "Study what General Pershing . . . did to terrorists when caught. There was no more Radical Islamic Terror for 35 years!"

In September 2017, President Trump tweeted that "[t]he travel ban into the United States should be far larger, tougher and more specific—but stupidly, that would not be politically correct!" Later that month, on September 24, 2017, President Trump issued [the current] Presidential Proclamation . . ., which restricts entry of certain nationals from six Muslim-majority countries. On November 29, 2017, President Trump "retweeted" three anti-Muslim videos, entitled "Muslim Destroys a Statue of Virgin Mary!", "Islamist mob pushes teenage boy off roof and beats him to death!", and "Muslim migrant beats up Dutch boy on crutches!" The content of these videos is highly inflammatory, and their titles are arguably misleading. [relocated footnote—eds.] Those videos were initially tweeted by a British political party whose mission is to oppose "all alien and destructive politic[al] or religious doctrines, including . . . Islam." When asked about these videos, the White House Deputy Press Secretary connected them to the Proclamation, responding that the "President has been talking about these security issues for years now, from the campaign trail to the White House" and "has addressed these issues with the travel order that he issued earlier this year and the companion proclamation."

As the majority correctly notes, "the issue before us is not whether to denounce" these offensive statements. Rather, the dispositive and narrow question here is whether a reasonable observer, presented with all "openly available data," the text and "historical context" of the Proclamation, and the "specific sequence of events" leading to it, would conclude that the primary purpose of the Proclamation is to disfavor Islam and its adherents by excluding them from the country. The answer is unquestionably yes.

Taking all the relevant evidence together, a reasonable observer would conclude that the Proclamation was driven primarily by anti-Muslim animus, rather than by the Government's asserted national-security justifications. Even before being sworn into office, then-candidate Trump stated that "Islam hates us," warned that "[w]e're having problems with the Muslims, and we're having problems with Muslims coming into the country," promised to enact a "total and complete shutdown of Muslims entering the United States," and instructed one of his advisers to find a "lega [l]" way to enact a Muslim ban, *id.,* at 125. The President continued to make similar statements well after his inauguration, as detailed above.

The Government urges us to disregard the President's campaign statements. . . . To the contrary, courts must consider "the historical background of the decision under challenge, the specific series of events leading to the enactment or official policy in question, and the legislative or administrative history." *Church of Lukumi Babalu Aye, Inc. v. Hialeah,* 508 U.S. 520, 540 (1993) (opinion of KENNEDY, J.). Moreover, President Trump and his advisers have repeatedly acknowledged that the Proclamation and its predecessors are an outgrowth of the President's campaign statements. For example, just last November, the Deputy White House Press Secretary reminded the media that the Proclamation addresses "issues" the President has been talking about "for years," including on "the campaign trail." In any case, as the Fourth Circuit correctly recognized, even without relying on any of the President's campaign statements, a reasonable observer would conclude that the Proclamation was enacted for the impermissible purpose of disfavoring Muslims. [relocated footnote — eds.]

Moreover, despite several opportunities to do so, President Trump has never disavowed any of his prior statements about Islam. Instead, he has continued to make remarks that a reasonable observer would view as an unrelenting attack on the Muslim religion and its followers. Given President Trump's failure to correct the reasonable perception of his apparent hostility toward the Islamic faith, it is unsurprising that the President's lawyers have, at every step in the lower courts, failed in their attempts to launder the Proclamation of its discriminatory taint. Notably, the Court recently found less pervasive official expressions of hostility and the failure to disavow them to be constitutionally significant. Cf. *Masterpiece Cakeshop, Ltd. v. Colorado Civil Rights Comm'n,* 584 U.S. ____, ____ (2018) (slip op., at 18) ("The official expressions of hostility to religion in some of the commissioners' comments — comments that were not disavowed at the Commission or by the State at any point in the proceedings that led to the affirmance of the order — were inconsistent with what the Free Exercise Clause requires"). It should find the same here.

Ultimately, what began as a policy explicitly "calling for a total and complete shutdown of Muslims entering the United States" has since morphed into a "Proclamation" putatively based on national-security concerns. But this new window dressing cannot conceal an unassailable fact: the words of the President and his advisers create the strong perception that the Proclamation is contaminated by impermissible discriminatory animus against Islam and its followers.

II

[T]he majority accepts that invitation and incorrectly applies a watered-down legal standard in an effort to short circuit plaintiffs' Establishment Clause claim. . . .

[*Kleindienst v.*] *Mandel* held that when the Executive Branch provides "a facially legitimate and bona fide reason" for denying a visa, "courts will neither look behind the exercise of that discretion, nor test it by balancing its justification." In his controlling concurrence in *Kerry v. Din,* 576 U.S. ____ (2015), JUSTICE KENNEDY applied *Mandel* 's holding and elaborated that courts can " 'look behind' the Government's exclusion of" a foreign national if there is "an affirmative showing of bad faith on the part of the consular officer who denied [the] visa." The extent to which *Mandel* and *Din* apply at all to this case is unsettled, and there is good reason to think they do not.

Mandel and *Din* are readily distinguishable from this case for a number of reasons. First, *Mandel* and *Din* each involved a constitutional challenge to an Executive Branch decision to exclude a single foreign national under a specific statutory ground of inadmissibility. Here, by contrast, President Trump is not exercising his discretionary authority to determine the admission or exclusion of a particular foreign national. He promulgated an executive order affecting millions of individuals on a categorical basis. Second, *Mandel* and *Din* did not purport to establish the framework for adjudicating cases (like this one) involving claims that the Executive Branch violated the Establishment Clause by acting pursuant to an unconstitutional purpose. Applying *Mandel* 's narrow standard of review to such a claim would run contrary to this Court's repeated admonition that "[f]acial neutrality is not determinative" in the Establishment Clause context. *Lukumi.* [T]he majority's passing invocation of *Fiallo v. Bell,* 430 U.S. 787 (1977), is misplaced. *Fiallo,* unlike this case, addressed a constitutional challenge to a statute enacted by Congress, not an order of the President. *Fiallo*'s application of *Mandel* says little about whether *Mandel*'s narrow standard of review applies to the unilateral executive proclamation promulgated under the circumstances of this case. Finally, even assuming that *Mandel* and *Din* apply here, they would not preclude us from looking behind the face of the Proclamation because plaintiffs have made "an affirmative showing of bad faith," *Din,* by the President who, among other things, instructed his subordinates to find a "lega[l]" way to enact a Muslim ban. [relocated footnote — eds.]

Indeed, even the Government agreed at oral argument that where the Court confronts a situation involving "all kinds of denigrating comments about" a particular religion and a subsequent policy that is designed with the purpose of disfavoring that religion but that "dot[s] all the i's and . . . cross[es] all the t's," *Mandel* would not "pu[t]" an end to judicial review of that set of facts."

In light of the Government's suggestion "that it may be appropriate here for the inquiry to extend beyond the facial neutrality of the order," the majority rightly declines to apply *Mandel*'s "narrow standard of review" and "assume [s] that we may look behind the face of the Proclamation." In doing so, however, the Court, without explanation or precedential support, limits its review of the Proclamation to rational-basis scrutiny. [But] in other Establishment Clause cases, including those involving claims of religious animus or discrimination, this Court has applied a more stringent standard of review.[6] As explained above, the Proclamation is plainly unconstitutional under that heightened standard. See *supra,* at 10-13.

The majority [argues that] this Court's Establishment Clause precedents do not apply to cases involving "immigration policies, diplomatic sanctions, and military actions." But just because the Court has not confronted the precise situation at hand does not render these cases (or the principles they announced) inapplicable. Moreover, . . . the majority itself fails to cite any "authority for its proposition" that a more probing review is inappropriate in a case like this one, where United States citizens allege that the Executive has violated the Establishment Clause by issuing a sweeping executive order motivated by animus. In any event, even if there is no prior case directly on point, it is clear from our precedent that "[w]hatever power the United States Constitution envisions for the Executive" in the context of national security and foreign affairs, "it most assuredly envisions a role for all three branches when individual liberties are at stake." *Hamdi v. Rumsfeld,* 542 U.S. 507, 536 (2004) (plurality opinion). This

Court's Establishment Clause precedents require that, if a reasonable observer would understand an executive action to be driven by discriminatory animus, the action be invalidated. *McCreary*. That reasonable-observer inquiry includes consideration of the Government's asserted justifications for its actions. The Government's invocation of a national-security justification, however, does not mean that the Court should close its eyes to other relevant information. Deference is different from unquestioning acceptance. Thus, what is "far more problematic" in this case is the majority's apparent willingness to throw the Establishment Clause out the window and forgo any meaningful constitutional review at the mere mention of a national-security concern. [relocated footnote—eds.]

But even under rational-basis review, the Proclamation must fall. That is so because the Proclamation is "'divorced from any factual context from which we could discern a relationship to legitimate state interests,' and 'its sheer breadth [is] so discontinuous with the reasons offered for it'" that the policy is " 'inexplicable by anything but animus.'" *Romer*; see also *Cleburne* (recognizing that classifications predicated on discriminatory animus can never be legitimate because the Government has no legitimate interest in exploiting "mere negative attitudes, or fear" toward a disfavored group). The President's statements, which the majority utterly fails to address in its legal analysis, strongly support the conclusion that the Proclamation was issued to express hostility toward Muslims and exclude them from the country. Given the overwhelming record evidence of anti-Muslim animus, it simply cannot be said that the Proclamation has a legitimate basis.

The majority insists that the Proclamation furthers two interrelated national-security interests: "preventing entry of nationals who cannot be adequately vetted and inducing other nations to improve their practices." But the Court offers insufficient support for its view "that the entry suspension has a legitimate grounding in [those] national security concerns, quite apart from any religious hostility." Indeed, even a cursory review of the Government's asserted national-security rationale reveals that the Proclamation is nothing more than a " 'religious gerrymander.' " *Lukumi*.

[T]he Proclamation, just like its predecessors, overwhelmingly targets Muslim-majority nations. Given the record here, including all the President's statements linking the Proclamation to his apparent hostility toward Muslims, it is of no moment that the Proclamation also includes minor restrictions on two non-Muslim majority countries, North Korea and Venezuela, or that the Government has removed a few Muslim-majority countries from the list of covered countries since EO-1 was issued. Consideration of the entire record supports the conclusion that the inclusion of North Korea and Venezuela, and the removal of other countries, simply reflect subtle efforts to start "talking territory instead of Muslim," precisely so the Executive Branch could evade criticism or legal consequences for the Proclamation's otherwise clear targeting of Muslims. The Proclamation's effect on North Korea and Venezuela, for example, is insubstantial, if not entirely symbolic. A prior sanctions order already restricts entry of North Korean nationals, and the Proclamation targets only a handful of

Venezuelan government officials and their immediate family members. As such, the President's inclusion of North Korea and Venezuela does little to mitigate the anti-Muslim animus that permeates the Proclamation.

The majority next contends that the Proclamation "reflects the results of a worldwide review process undertaken by multiple Cabinet officials." [T]he worldwide review does little to break the clear connection between the Proclamation and the President's anti-Muslim statements. For "[n]o matter how many officials affix their names to it, the Proclamation rests on a rotten foundation." The President campaigned on a promise to implement a "total and complete shutdown of Muslims" entering the country, translated that campaign promise into a concrete policy, and made several statements linking that policy (in its various forms) to anti-Muslim animus.

Ignoring all this, the majority empowers the President to hide behind an administrative review process that the Government refuses to disclose to the public. Furthermore, evidence of which we can take judicial notice indicates that the multiagency review process could not have been very thorough. Ongoing litigation under the Freedom of Information Act shows that the September 2017 report the Government produced after its review process was a mere 17 pages. That the Government's analysis of the vetting practices of hundreds of countries boiled down to such a short document raises serious questions about the legitimacy of the President's proclaimed national-security rationale.

Beyond that, Congress has already addressed the national-security concerns supposedly undergirding the Proclamation through an "extensive and complex" framework governing "immigration and alien status." . . . In addition to vetting rigorously any individuals seeking admission to the United States, the Government also rigorously vets the information-sharing and identity-management systems of other countries. . . . Put simply, Congress has already erected a statutory scheme that fulfills the putative national-security interests the Government now puts forth to justify the Proclamation. Tellingly, the Government remains wholly unable to articulate any credible national-security interest that would go unaddressed by the current statutory scheme absent the Proclamation. The Government also offers no evidence that this current vetting scheme, which involves a highly searching consideration of individuals required to obtain visas for entry into the United States and a highly searching consideration of which countries are eligible for inclusion in the Visa Waiver Program, is inadequate to achieve the Proclamation's proclaimed objectives of "preventing entry of nationals who cannot be adequately vetted and inducing other nations to improve their [vetting and information-sharing] practices."

For many of these reasons, several former national-security officials from both political parties — including former Secretary of State Madeleine Albright, former State Department Legal Adviser John Bellinger III, former Central Intelligence Agency Director John Brennan, and former Director of National Intelligence James Clapper — have advised that the Proclamation and its predecessor orders "do not advance the national-security or foreign policy interests of the United States, and in fact do serious harm to those interests."

Moreover, the Proclamation purports to mitigate national-security risks by excluding nationals of countries that provide insufficient information to vet their nationals. Yet, as plaintiffs explain, the Proclamation broadly denies immigrant visas to all nationals of those countries, including those whose admission would likely not implicate these information deficiencies (*e.g.,* infants, or nationals of countries included in the Proclamation who are long-term residents of and traveling from a country not covered by the Proclamation). In addition, the Proclamation permits certain nationals from the countries named in the Proclamation to obtain nonimmigrant visas, which undermines the Government's assertion that it does not already have the capacity and sufficient information to vet these individuals adequately.

Equally unavailing is the majority's reliance on the Proclamation's waiver program. As several *amici* thoroughly explain, there is reason to suspect that the Proclamation's waiver program is nothing more than a sham. The remote possibility of obtaining a waiver pursuant to an ad hoc, discretionary, and seemingly arbitrary process scarcely demonstrates that the Proclamation is rooted in a genuine concern for national security.

In sum, none of the features of the Proclamation highlighted by the majority supports the Government's claim that the Proclamation is genuinely and primarily rooted in a legitimate national-security interest. What the unrebutted evidence actually shows is that a reasonable observer would conclude, quite easily, that the primary purpose and function of the Proclamation is to disfavor Islam by banning Muslims from entering our country.

III

[P]laintiffs are likely to succeed on the merits of their Establishment Clause claim. [They have also shown] that they are "likely to suffer irreparable harm in the absence of preliminary relief," that "the balance of equities tips in [their] favor," and that "an injunction is in the public interest."

First, . . . plaintiffs have adduced substantial evidence showing that the Proclamation will result in "a multitude of harms that are not compensable with monetary damages and that are irreparable — among them, prolonged separation from family members, constraints to recruiting and retaining students and faculty members to foster diversity and quality within the University community, and the diminished membership of the [Muslim] Association."

Second, plaintiffs have demonstrated that the balance of the equities tips in their favor. Against plaintiffs' concrete allegations of serious harm, the Government advances only nebulous national-security concerns. Although national security is unquestionably an issue of paramount public importance, it is not "a talisman" that the Government can use "to ward off inconvenient claims — a 'label' used to 'cover a multitude of sins.'" That is especially true here, because, as noted, the Government's other statutory tools, including the existing rigorous individualized vetting process, already address the Proclamation's purported national-security concerns.

Finally, plaintiffs and their *amici* have convincingly established that "an injunction is in the public interest." As explained by the scores of *amici* who have filed briefs in support of plaintiffs, the Proclamation has deleterious effects on our higher education system; national security; healthcare; artistic culture; and the Nation's technology industry and overall economy. Accordingly, the Court of Appeals correctly affirmed, in part, the District Court's preliminary injunction.

IV

The First Amendment stands as a bulwark against official religious prejudice and embodies our Nation's deep commitment to religious plurality and tolerance. . . . Instead of vindicating those principles, today's decision tosses them aside. In holding that the First Amendment gives way to an executive policy that a reasonable observer would view as motivated by animus against Muslims, the majority opinion upends this Court's precedent, repeats tragic mistakes of the past, and denies countless individuals the fundamental right of religious liberty.

Just weeks ago, the Court rendered its decision in *Masterpiece Cakeshop,* 584 U.S. ____, [involving a baker who refused to bake a wedding cake for a gay couple,] which applied the bedrock principles of religious neutrality and tolerance in considering a First Amendment challenge to government action. See *id.,* at ____ (slip op., at 17) ("The Constitution 'commits government itself to religious tolerance, and upon even slight suspicion that proposals for state intervention stem from animosity to religion or distrust of its practices, all officials must pause to remember their own high duty to the Constitution and to the rights it secures'". Those principles should apply equally here. In both instances, the question is whether a government actor exhibited tolerance and neutrality in reaching a decision that affects individuals' fundamental religious freedom. But unlike in *Masterpiece,* where a state civil rights commission was found to have acted without "the neutrality that the Free Exercise Clause requires," *id.,* at ____ (slip op., at 17), the government actors in this case will not be held accountable for breaching the First Amendment's guarantee of religious neutrality and tolerance. Unlike in *Masterpiece,* where the majority considered the state commissioners' statements about religion to be persuasive evidence of unconstitutional government action, the majority here completely sets aside the President's charged statements about Muslims as irrelevant. That holding erodes the foundational principles of religious tolerance that the Court elsewhere has so emphatically protected, and it tells members of minority religions in our country " 'that they are outsiders, not full members of the political community.' "

Today's holding is all the more troubling given the stark parallels between the reasoning of this case and that of *Korematsu v. United States,* 323 U.S. 214 (1944). In *Korematsu,* the Court gave "a pass [to] an odious, gravely injurious racial classification" authorized by an executive order. As here, the Government invoked an ill-defined national-security threat to justify an exclusionary policy of sweeping proportion. As here, the exclusion order was rooted in dangerous stereotypes about, *inter alia,* a particular group's supposed inability to assimilate and desire to harm the United States. As here, the Government was unwilling to reveal its own intelligence agencies' views of the alleged security concerns to the very citizens it purported to protect. And as here, there was strong evidence that impermissible hostility and animus motivated the Government's policy.

Although a majority of the Court in *Korematsu* was willing to uphold the Government's actions based on a barren invocation of national security, dissenting Justices warned of that decision's harm to our constitutional fabric. Justice Murphy recognized that there is a need for great deference to the Executive Branch in the context of national security, but cautioned that "it is essential that there be definite limits to [the government's] discretion," as "[i]ndividuals must not be left impoverished of their constitutional rights on a plea of military necessity that has neither substance nor support." Justice Jackson lamented that the Court's decision upholding the Government's policy would prove to be "a far more subtle blow to liberty than the promulgation of the order itself," for although the executive order was not likely to be long lasting, the Court's willingness to tolerate it would endure.

In the intervening years since *Korematsu,* our Nation has done much to leave its sordid legacy behind. See, *e.g.,* Civil Liberties Act of 1988, 50 U.S.C. App. § 4211 *et seq.* (setting forth remedies to individuals affected by the executive order at issue in *Korematsu*); Non–Detention Act of 1971, 18 U.S.C. § 4001(a) (forbidding the imprisonment or detention by the United States of any citizen absent an Act of Congress). Today, the Court takes the important step of finally overruling *Korematsu,* denouncing it as "gravely wrong the day it was decided." This formal repudiation of a shameful precedent is laudable and long overdue. But it does not make the majority's decision here acceptable or right. By blindly accepting the Government's misguided invitation to sanction a discriminatory policy motivated by animosity toward a disfavored group, all in the name of a superficial claim of national security, the Court redeploys the same dangerous logic underlying *Korematsu* and merely replaces one "gravely wrong" decision with another.

Our Constitution demands, and our country deserves, a Judiciary willing to hold the coordinate branches to account when they defy our most sacred legal commitments. Because the Court's decision today has failed in that respect, with profound regret, I dissent.

Discussion

1. *The plenary power doctrine and immigration exceptionalism.* One cannot understand the issues in *Trump v. Hawaii* apart from immigration law's unique status in the constitutional order. The current understanding of the federal government's power to regulate immigration stems from the plenary power doctrine that originated in the 19th century Chinese Exclusion Case, Chae Chan Ping v. United States, 130 U.S. 581, 609 (1889). This doctrine emerged only in the late 19th century; in the first hundred years of the country's history, the states played a much greater role in immigration regulation. See, e.g., Mayor of the City of New York v. Miln, 36 U.S. (11 Pet.) 102 (1837) (Casebook, p. 223). For an explanation of the rise of the plenary power doctrine, see Sarah H. Cleveland, Powers

Inherent In Sovereignty: Indians, Aliens, Territories, and the Nineteenth Century Origins of Plenary Power Over Foreign Affairs, 81 Tex. L. Rev. 1 (2002).

The plenary power doctrine is associated with two different ideas. The first is that Congress's power to regulate immigration does not come from any enumerated power in Article I, but rather is an "an incident of sovereignty belonging to the government of the United States." Chae Chan Ping, 130 U.S. at 609. This theory suggests that, notwithstanding the theory of limited and enumerated powers, the federal government of the United States is like that of any other nation, with the right to protect national sovereignty by enforcing its borders. (It is perhaps no accident that the plenary power doctrine emerges after the Civil War). This theory views the plenary power doctrine as a matter of *sovereignty*.

The second idea is that—with a few notable exceptions—courts have largely refrained from enforcing constitutional constraints on the federal government's enactment and enforcement of immigration laws. See, e.g., Fiallo v. Bell, 430 U.S. 787, 792 (1977) ("Our cases have long recognized the power to expel or exclude aliens as a fundamental sovereign attribute exercised by the Government's political departments largely immune from judicial control.") This theory of the plenary power doctrine is premised on the superior *competence* of the political branches over that of the judiciary in questions of immigration and foreign affairs.

Federal courts have often allowed the political branches to make classifications and distinctions in immigration enforcement that would almost certainly be unconstitutional if made by the states, or even if made by the federal government outside of the immigration context. As a result, standard-form equal protection doctrine does not apply. See generally Gabriel J. Chin, Segregation's Last Stronghold: Race Discrimination and the Constitutional Law of Immigration, 46 UCLA L. Rev. 1 (1998). In addition, the Court has not generally used the Bill of Rights to protect the rights of noncitizens who live *outside* the United States. See United States v. Verdugo–Urquidez, 494 U.S. 259, 269 (1990) (holding that the Fifth Amendment's protections do not extend to aliens outside the territorial boundaries of the United States). *Trump v. Hawaii* arises in this difficult context for the protection of the rights of aliens.

2. *The scope of the plenary power doctrine and the role of judicial scrutiny in immigration law.* There are at least two different explanations for judicial deference in immigration law. The stronger version holds that the Constitution's equality norms simply do not constrain the distinctions the political branches use in deciding who can enter the country. The federal government has broad power to make virtually any distinctions it wants about who gains entry to the country and who must leave—including, for example, on the basis of religion, race, or national origin. The Justice Department did not adopt this position in the travel ban litigation. In oral arguments before the courts of appeals, DOJ lawyers conceded that it would be unconstitutional for the government to exclude Muslims, as such, from entering the United States. And in the Supreme Court opinion itself, Chief Justice Roberts (and Justice Kennedy's concurrence) assumed that the government could violate the Establishment Clause.

The second version of the "plenary power" doctrine focuses on the role of courts: Although the Constitution may impose substantive constraints on the immigration power, the judiciary should not attempt to oversee the political branches or decide whether the political branches have violated the Constitution. This norm is very strong but it is not insuperable. See, e.g., Sessions v. Morales-Santana, 137 S.Ct.1678 (2017) (upholding an equal protection challenge in the face of a plenary power objection).[1] When courts consider claims of plenary power in the context of immigration law, courts generally apply a "presumption of regularity" and they accept at face value the Executive's representations of the basis for immigration restrictions. In the words of *Kleindienst v. Mandel,* "when the Executive exercises th[e] power [to exclude an alien] on the basis of a facially legitimate and bona fide reason, the courts will [not] look behind the exercise of that discretion."

3. *Litigation strategies for getting around the plenary power doctrine.* Although the plenary power doctrine is still very much alive, social change, political mobilization, globalization, and litigation strategies have put it under increasing pressure. The travel ban cases exemplify how constitutional doctrine in this area is being contested and reshaped in an era of globalization.

Plaintiffs attempting to chip away at the plenary power doctrine have tried two different strategies. First, they have used federal statutory claims and procedural objections to protect constitutional norms. Second, plaintiffs have tried to protect the rights of aliens through protecting the constitutional rights of *citizens and permanent resident aliens* who are affected by the immigration laws. This avoids having to argue that the Constitution applies outside the territory of the United States. We see both of these strategies in *Trump v. Hawaii*: an argument that the President has not made appropriate findings for the Proclamation and that the Proclamation violates the Establishment Clause because it evidences government disapproval of Islam and discriminates against Muslims in the United States.

Because, as noted above, courts do not apply standard-form equal protection doctrine to immigration restrictions, the plaintiffs in the travel ban litigation also tried to use various workarounds to bring equality ideas into the analysis.

The statutory argument was based on the antidiscrimination rule of § 1152(a)(1)(A) of the 1965 Immigration and Naturalization Act, which was passed contemporaneously with the 1964 Civil Rights Act and the 1965 Voting Act.[2] The plaintiffs also argued that the Trump Administration had not offered

---

1. In *Morales-Santana*, a federal statute made it more difficult for American fathers—as compared with American mothers—to transmit citizenship to their children born out of wedlock on foreign soil. In this case, which involved an explicit classification based on sex, the Court found an equal protection violation. But it remedied the constitutional inequality not by making it easier for American fathers to transmit citizenship, but by making it equally difficult for American mothers. Thus, it decided the case in a way that interfered as little as possible with Congress's political prerogatives. See Casebook at pp. 1323-26; cf. Kristin A. Collins, Equality, Sovereignty, and the Family in Morales-Santana, The Supreme Court—Comments, 131 Harv. L. Rev. 170, 204-08, 221 (2017).

2. See Cristina M. Rodriguez, Immigration and the Civil Rights Agenda, 6 Stan. J. C.R. & C.L. 125, 127 (2010) ("The 1965 reforms of the INA that finally abolished [racially discriminatory immigration] quotas emerged from the political and cultural milieu that produced the Civil Rights

factual findings to justify its Executive Order, and that the process by which the decision was made was procedurally irregular. Demonstrating a poor fit between means and ends, noting lack of adequate explanation, and emphasizing procedural irregularities are standard ways that courts show invidious motivation, or otherwise establish impermissible distinctions, in equal protection doctrine.

The plaintiffs' constitutional argument was based on the Establishment Clause, which has important overlaps with equality doctrines under the Fourteenth and Fifth Amendments. First, it forbids the government from preferring one religion over another, or religion over nonreligion; it also forbids signaling that some people are disfavored because of their religious identity, beliefs or practices. Second, as in equal protection law, one can show a violation of these norms by showing an intent to discriminate on the basis of religion. Third, modern Establishment Clause doctrine often focuses on the social meaning of government action, by asking whether a reasonable observer would view the government as endorsing (or disfavoring) a particular religion or religion in general. This inquiry is similar to the way the Court has treated animus doctrine in gay rights cases such as *Romer v. Evans* and *United States v. Windsor*.

4. *Taking Trump seriously but not literally*. Chief Justice Roberts well recognizes that President Trump had made many hostile remarks about Muslims in public both before and after his election. So it was not possible for the Court to pretend that there was no evidence of prejudice. Note carefully how Roberts deals with that problem in resolving the issues in the case.

Consider how Roberts states the facts of the case: he begins with the third of President Trump's executive orders, offering only a brief mention of the two earlier orders. The dissent, by contrast, begins the story with the 2016 campaign. Roberts' framing focuses on an order that had been drafted and revised as a result of consultation among many different government actors. (Ironically, the reason why the third executive order appeared more professional than the earlier two was that the lower courts repeatedly forced the Executive Branch to respond to their objections.) The dissent's story, by contrast, suggests that the travel ban's origins were in demagogic politics; the original Executive order, EO-1, was hastily drafted with little professional advice, no inter-agency consultation, and no serious attempt at discovering the facts. Roberts' version of the facts focuses on a history of consultation, agency findings, and professional opinions which informed the President's judgment. The dissent's version of the facts focuses on a continuous pattern of provocative statements and tweets by the head of the Executive Branch, the President of the United States, who did not seem to care how the order was drafted as long as it achieved its original purpose.

How does the majority deal with the problem of these statements and tweets? Several lower courts judges and legal commentators argued that Trump's campaign statements could simply be disregarded because they were not made in

---

Act of 1964 and the Voting Rights Act of 1965 and were defended by members of Congress as realizations of the anti-discrimination aspirations of the era.").

his official capacity as President. Consider why this might make sense from the standpoint of constitutional law. One possibility is that campaign statements are unreliable evidence of intentions. Perhaps candidates will say things they don't really believe to get power but once they take office they will reveal their actual beliefs. A second possibility is that campaign statements do not reflect the views of the Administration as a whole. (Why is this relevant if the President is the head of the Executive Branch?) A third possibility has nothing to do with the reliability of the evidence. Instead, it argues that campaigns are often messy, dirty affairs, and politicians should get a fresh start once they take office, so that they are not hamstrung by what they had to say to get into office. One of the problems with these arguments is that Trump didn't seem to change his behavior very much after he became President. Instead, he understood that his supporters liked his blunt views about Muslims and he played to his base repeatedly once in office.

Roberts takes a different approach to the problem. He begins by asserting that "the issue before us is not whether to denounce the statements." What does he mean by this? (Note that the Court has no problem denouncing the Japanese internment later in the opinion. Is the difference that these events are safely in the past and do not involve a sitting president?)

Next, Roberts remarks that "we must consider not only the statements of a particular President, but also the authority of the Presidency itself." Thus, Roberts seems to be saying, there cannot be a "Trump discount" in construing the policies of this Administration, with judges offering less deference to Trump than they would to other presidents. Do you agree that courts should not decide cases based on their estimate of whether a given president is markedly different from other presidents in terms of competence, public-spiritedness, venality, rationality, or intelligence?

Roberts believes that whatever rule the Court applies, it cannot be one specially crafted for Trump, but must be a rule that could apply to any President, and, more important, to the entire Executive Branch — which is composed of many people, including diplomatic, military, and legal professionals.

One reason for not focusing on Trump's own statements, or applying a "Trump discount" to his administration's decisions, is that Trump is the head of a large bureaucracy that forms the Executive Branch of government. What conception of executive decision making does Roberts presuppose here? Does he assume that President Trump was not actually the primary mover and final decider with respect to the travel ban? Does he assume that professionals in his Administration reached a similar judgment about the need for the policy free from any bias towards Muslims? Suppose the President ordered his employees to come up with an exclusion policy because he harbors a prejudice against Muslims, or because he found that it was a winning issue during the election and believed that it would play well with elements of his political base who are hostile to Muslims. Nevertheless, he told his employees to eliminate any facial discrimination against Muslims so that the travel ban would appear legally innocuous. Should this be sufficient for the policy to pass muster?

At oral argument, the Solicitor General Noel Francisco emphasized that the travel ban arose out of routine and professional Executive branch deliberation rather than from the arbitrary decision of a rogue President. Consider this remarkable exchange with Justice Kagan:

> JUSTICE KAGAN: [L]et's say in some future time a . . . President gets elected who is a vehement anti-Semite . . . and says all kinds of denigrating comments about Jews and provokes a lot of resentment and hatred over the course of a campaign and in his presidency and, in the course of that, asks his staff or his cabinet members . . . to issue recommendations so that he can issue a proclamation of this kind, and they dot all the i's and they cross all the t's. And what emerges . . . is a proclamation that says no one shall enter from Israel. . . . Do you say [Kleindienst v.] Mandel puts an end to judicial review of that set of facts?
>
> GENERAL FRANCISCO: No, Your Honor, I don't say Mandel puts an end to it. . . . Mandel would be the starting point of the analysis, because it does involve the exclusion of aliens. . . . [I]f his cabinet were to actually come to him and say, Mr. President, there is honestly a national security risk here and you have to act, I think then that the President would be allowed to follow that advice even if in his private heart of hearts he also harbored animus. . . .
>
> Given that Israel happens to be one of the country's closest allies in the war against terrorism, it's not clear to me that you actually could satisfy. . . Mandel's rational basis standard on that, unless it truly were based . . . on a cabinet-level recommendation that was about national security.
>
> JUSTICE KAGAN: General . . . this is a[n] out-of-the-box kind of President in my hypothetical. . . . (Laughter.)
>
> GENERAL FRANCISCO: We — we — we don't have those, Your Honor.[3]

Should the result be any different if the President is "out-of-the-box"?

5. *From facial validity to rational basis?* Note how Roberts deals with *Kleindienst v. Mandel.* He does not simply apply its test of whether there is a "facially legitimate and bona fide" explanation for the Proclamation. Instead, he accepts (as did the Solicitor General) that the Court may have to look behind the face of the policy. Why concede this point? One possibility is that Roberts felt constrained by the factual record in the case. This is not a situation in which the Justices might merely *suspect* that the President is prejudiced; rather the record provides evidence that he is prejudiced against Muslims and that he traded on prejudice against Muslims (and other minority groups) to get elected.

Having conceded that the Court should look behind the policy and engage in judicial scrutiny, Roberts chooses the very lowest level of scrutiny, the rational basis test of Williamson v. Lee Optical, which makes no inquiry into actual motivations, postulates public-spirited purposes even for suspicions legislation passed in suspicious circumstances, and asks if there is any conceivable set of facts that might justify the choices the government has made. What justifies this choice of the standard of review? (Note Chief Justice Roberts' citation to

---

3. Trump v. Hawaii, Oral Argument Transcript at 16-18.

Railroad Retirement Board v. Fritz (Casebook, p. 567), a case in which Congress had been bamboozled into voting for a bill whose consequences it did not fully understand; the Court nevertheless held that the statute passed the rational basis test.) Rational basis used this way effectively eliminates any inquiry into *actual* motivations, which, of course, is the central issue that plaintiffs were trying to raise. Thus, modifying *Kleindienst* to include a rational basis inquiry doesn't change the result.

Of course, standard-form Establishment Clause doctrine does not apply rational basis. Instead it asks whether a government policy has the purpose or effect of endorsing or disfavoring a particular religion or religion in general. Thus, it focuses on actual motivations. Moreover, the government's purpose must be "genuine, not a sham, and not merely secondary to a religious objective." McCreary County v. ACLU of Ky., 545 U.S. 844 (2005).

Roberts explains that such judicial scrutiny is best designed for cases involving domestic laws and policies, and not decisions about "immigration policies, diplomatic sanctions, and military actions." What justifies this distinction? Remember that a classic justification for heightened scrutiny (elaborated in footnote four of *Carolene Products*) is democratic legitimacy. If government officials have acted with prejudice toward discrete and insular minorities, their actions lack democratic legitimacy. Are concerns of democratic legitimacy less relevant or important where the subject matter is "immigration policies, diplomatic sanctions, and military actions"? Or is Roberts' point that courts are simply less competent to pass on these questions?

6. *Rational basis, no bite.* Roberts recognizes that there is another version of the rational basis test, "rational basis with a bite," that *does* focus on whether a policy is based on irrational prejudice (*Cleburne*) or animus (*Romer v. Evans*). However, Roberts does not apply this test in the way it was applied in United States v. Windsor, 133 S. Ct. 2675 (2013), which struck down the Defense of Marriage Act (see Casebook pp. 1570-74). Roberts says that the Proclamation is constitutional because "[i]t cannot be said that it is impossible to 'discern a relationship to legitimate state interests' or that the policy is 'inexplicable by anything but animus.'" Yet *Windsor* struck down a ban on federal benefits for same-sex marriages even though the government had identified a series of legitimate state interests; rather the case turned on the majority's belief that the law was motivated by anti-gay animus.

7. *Justice Kennedy washes his hands.* Note Justice Kennedy's concurrence, which provides the crucial fifth vote. He argues that although courts will not interfere with Executive Branch foreign policy decisions, Executive Branch officials also take an oath to uphold the Constitution, and they have a duty not to make decisions based on unconstitutional motives. In fact, Kennedy says, it is precisely because courts will not second-guess government officials' decisions in the area of foreign policy that they must be especially careful not to violate the Constitution. Does Kennedy offer any way of reining in Presidents who do not take their oaths seriously? Or is his point that this must be left to electoral politics?

What do you make of Justice Kennedy's citation to *Romer v. Evans* and his statement that "Whether judicial proceedings may properly continue in this case, in light of the substantial deference that is and must be accorded to the Executive in the conduct of foreign affairs, and in light of today's decision, is a matter to be addressed in the first instance on remand"? Does this leave the door open to further litigation and discovery on the question of the President's "animosity to a religion"?[4]

Justice Kennedy announced his retirement at the end of June 2018, and was replaced by Justice Brett Kavanaugh. It is not yet clear what the newly constituted Court will do with the animus doctrine, as developed in his decisions in *Romer* and *Windsor*.

8. *What does it mean to overrule* Korematsu? Both the majority and the dissent compare the travel ban decision to *Korematsu*. Justice Sotomayor's dissent argues that the Court in *Hawaii v. Trump* failed to stand up to prejudice, and was cowed by claims of national security, just as it had been in *Korematsu*. Thus, through the very act of overruling *Korematsu*, the Court was legitimating new forms of racial and religious discrimination.

Chief Justice Roberts makes two points. First, he denounces *Korematsu*, which he says, "has been overruled in the court of history, and—to be clear—has no place in law under the Constitution."

Second, and perhaps more important, he distinguishes *Korematsu*, arguing that it "has nothing to do with this case." *Korematsu* involved "[t]he forcible relocation of U.S. citizens to concentration camps, solely and explicitly on the basis of race," whereas Trump's Proclamation is "a facially neutral policy denying certain foreign nationals the privilege of admission. The entry suspension is an act that is well within executive authority and could have been taken by any other President." And because "the Government has set forth a sufficient national security justification to survive rational basis review," the Court will uphold the suspension.

President Roosevelt's Executive Order 9066 was facially neutral as to race and nationality: it simply gave the military the authority to designate areas "from which any or all persons may be excluded." However, General DeWitt's proclamations based on that order were directed at "all persons of Japanese ancestry."

Note that *Korematsu* involved both the detention of both Japanese-American citizens *and* Japanese-American resident aliens. Roberts' description of the vice of *Korematsu* only refers to citizens. Does this mean that *Korematsu* is still good law if the government decides to round up and detain Muslim non-citizens present in the United States?

One of the ironies of Roberts' dual move—denouncing *Korematsu* and distinguishing it—is that the "overruling" of *Korematsu* is purely dicta, because,

---

4. For an argument to this effect, see Noah Feldman, Take Trump's Travel Ban Back to Court, Bloomberg News, June 29, 2018, https://www.bloomberg.com/view/articles/2018-06-29/take-trump-s-travel-ban-back-to-court (discussing arguments by Owen Fiss).

according to Roberts, the case is legally irrelevant to the issues presented in Trump v. Hawaii.

9. *The court of history.* Roberts says that Korematsu "has been overruled by the court of history." What is the relationship between the "court of history" and the Supreme Court of the United States? The theory of interpretation presupposed by this metaphor is that, in the long run, later generations decide whether earlier generations have correctly interpreted the Constitution. Yet Roberts also says that *Korematsu* was "wrong the day it was decided," so, presumably, it was not necessary to wait for history's judgment.

10. "Korematsu *has nothing to do with this case.*" Why does *Korematsu* "ha[ve] nothing to do" with Trump v. Hawaii?[5] Consider the following possibilities:

1. *Korematsu* (and related decisions such as *Hirabayashi v. United States*, 320 U.S. 81 (1943)) involved race, whereas *Trump* involves religion.

2. *Korematsu* and *Hirabayashi* involved Japanese-American citizens and resident aliens, whereas *Trump* involved aliens seeking to enter the United States.

3. *Korematsu* and *Hirabayashi* involved curfews and detention, whereas *Trump* involves exclusion from the United States and the separation of families.

4. *Korematsu* and *Hirabayashi* were justified on national security grounds but the military orders in question involved an explicit categorization based on race, whereas *Trump* is justified on national security grounds but it involves a facially neutral rule that survives rational basis scrutiny. It is true that the Court generally treat invidious motivation as being as unconstitutional as facial classification (See Washington v. Davis, which requires a showing of intention, and *Masterpiece Cakeshop*, decided this Term, in which the Court held that Colorado had violated religious neutrality.) However, in *Trump*, Justice Roberts argues that the Court should not inquire into unconstitutional motivation because "[i]t cannot be said that it is impossible to 'discern a relationship to legitimate state interests' or that the policy is 'inexplicable by anything but animus.'"

What do you make of these possible distinctions?

One may assume that a well-trained lawyer can demonstrate that almost any contemporary government action defended on grounds of national security these days is distinguishable from *Korematsu* and *Hirabayashi*. (Consider, as examples, the actions of the Bush and Obama administrations in dealing with terrorist suspects: the establishment of Guantanamo Bay as (in effect) a law-free zone, the use of waterboarding and other "enhanced interrogation techniques," and the use of drones.) That said, do *Korematsu* and *Hirabayashi* have any other lessons for contemporary decisionmakers about national security and constitutional values?

5. See Joseph Fishkin, Why was Korematsu Wrong, Balkinization, June 26, 2018, https://balkin.blogspot.com/2018/06/why-was-korematsu-wrong.html ; Richard Primus, The Travel Ban and Inter-Branch Conflict, Take Care, June 26, 2018, https://takecareblog.com/blog/the-travel-ban-and-inter-branch-conflict.

Chapter 8

Sex Equality

Insert on p. 1273 immediately before Note: The Nineteenth Amendment.

Note: Can The Equal Rights Amendment Be Ratified Today?

The Equal Rights Amendment, first proposed in Congress in 1923, was approved by both houses of Congress in 1972 and sent to the states. The text of the 1972 proposal reads:

Section 1. Equality of rights under the law shall not be denied or abridged by the United States or by any state on account of sex.
Section 2. The Congress shall have the power to enforce, by appropriate legislation, the provisions of this article.
Section 3. This amendment shall take effect two years after the date of ratification.

The joint Congressional resolution sending the proposal to the states placed a seven-year deadline on ratification. Between 1972 and 1977, 35 state legislatures ratified the ERA. However, as discussed in the Casebook (pp. 1267-68) the New Right, led by Phyllis Schlafly, made opposition to the ERA a signature issue, and the ratifications stalled. Congress extended the deadline to 1982, but no more states ratified during the extended period.

The ERA gathered renewed interest in during the 2010s. In 2008, a Facebook page dedicated to support for the ERA began discussing sexist responses to Hillary Clinton's candidacy for the Democratic nomination for President in 2008 and protesting the Supreme Court's pay equity decision in Lilly Ledbetter v Goodyear Tire & Rubber Co., 550 U.S. 618 (2007).[1] After Donald Trump became President, prompting a national Women's March in January of 2017, focus on the Amendment's ratification intensified.[2] Shortly thereafter, in March of 2017,

---

1. For the ERA Facebook page, see https://www.facebook.com/ERAusa/.
2. For short history of the recent mobilization, see Dahlia Lithwick,The ERA is Back: The '70s-era constitutional amendment could be the perfect remedy for the #MeToo era, Slate, April 23, 2018, https://slate.com/news-and-politics/2018/04/the-equal-rights-amendment-could-be-the-perfect-remedy-for-the-metoo-era.html; The Equal Rights Amendment: Unfinished Business for the Constitution, http://www.equalrightsamendment.org/; Jessica Newirth, Equal Means Equal: Why the Time for an Equal Rights Amendment Is Now (2015).

Nevada's Legislature ratified the 1972 proposal. Illinois followed in 2018. This brought the number of states to 37, one short of the 38 required for ratification.[3] However, 5 states had rescinded their ratifications in the 1970s: Nebraska (1973), Tennessee (1974), Idaho (1977), Kentucky (1978), and South Dakota (1979).[4] This raises the question of whether six more states — rather than a single one — are needed to ratify.[5]

If a 38th state (other than those mentioned above) ratifies, what will be the legal effect?

Discussion

1. *The role of time limits.* Can states disregard time limits set by Congress? One might distinguish between time limits which appear in the actual text of the proposal (call these textual time limits), and time limits which appear only in the congressional resolution that sends the proposed amendment to the states (call these proposal time limits). Amendments 18 and 20-22 have textual time limits; later amendments (with the notable exception of the 27th, to be discussed shortly) have included time limits in the Congressional proposal.

One might argue that while states cannot ratify a proposed amendment which, by its own terms, expires on a certain date, they need not be bound by time limits that appear only in the congressional proposal that accompanies the text. "It was in the resolving clause, but it wasn't a part of the amendment that was proposed by Congress," the Nevada bill's chief sponsor observed. "That's why the time limit is irrelevant."[6]

Article V specifies that "The Congress, whenever two thirds of both houses shall deem it necessary, *shall propose amendments* to this Constitution." Such proposals "shall be valid to all intents and purposes, as part of this Constitution, when ratified by the legislatures of three fourths of the several states, or by conventions in three fourths thereof, *as the one or the other mode of ratification may be proposed by the Congress.*"

Defenders of Congressional prerogatives might argue that this language gives Congress complete power to decide both the nature of the proposal and the conditions under which ratification becomes effective.

---

3. Robinson Woodward-Burns, *The Equal Rights Amendment is One State from Ratification. Now What?*, WASH. POST (June 20, 2018), https://wapo.st/2M2Yj1m.

4. Thomas H. Neale, Cong. Res. Serv., *The Proposed Equal Rights Amendment: Contemporary Ratification Issues*, (July 28, 2017), http://lwvnc.org/wp-content/uploads/2017/09/2017-CRS-ERA-Ratification-Contemporary-Issues-7-28-2017.pdf.

5. See Rachel Frank, *Previewing the ERA Debates*, BALKINIZATION, https://balkin.blogspot.com/2018/06/previewing-era-debates.html, on which this discussion note is based.

6. Colin Dwyer & Carrie Kaufman, Nevada Ratifies The Equal Rights Amendment . . . 35 Years After The Deadline, Morning Edition, National Public Radio, March 21, 2017, https://www.npr.org/sections/thetwo-way/2017/03/21/520962541/nevada-on-cusp-of-ratifying-equal-rights-amendment-35-years-after-deadline.

Defenders of state prerogatives might respond that the language does no such thing: Congress merely has the power to decide whether ratifications will be by state legislatures or by state conventions; hence, it may not impose additional conditions. For this reason, the 1982 extension was completely unnecessary, and its expiration was irrelevant.

In Dillon v. Gloss, 256 U.S. 368 (1921), the Supreme Court held that Congress had the power to impose time limits on a proposed amendment to the Constitution, and that seven years was a reasonable requirement. (*Dillion* involved the Eighteenth Amendment, which included time limits in the text of the amendment itself). Conversely, the Supreme Court held in *Coleman v. Miller*, 307 U.S. 433 (1939), that if Congress chooses not to add time limits, proposals remain alive indefinitely. The Court argued that the question of whether ratification is timely is a political question, left to Congress's judgment. (See Casebook pp. 526-28) *Coleman* involved a proposed Child Labor Amendment (which would have given Congress the power to pass laws regulating child labor); both the Child Labor Amendment and the Nineteenth Amendment contained no time limits, unlike Amendments 18 and 20-26.

Note that if one accepts that Congress gets to make decisions about ratification, it might also follow that Congress has the power to extend the deadline if it chooses. That would mean that the 1982 extension was valid. But what if a state (such as Nevada and Illinois) ratifies after the extension has expired? Again, there are several possibilities. The ratifications after 1982 might be invalid. Or Congress may accept these ratifications as valid retroactively, if it passes a new joint resolution promulgating the ratification of the new amendment. (Query: would such a promulgating resolution require a two-thirds vote of both houses or only a simple majority? Note that the text of Article V says nothing about Congress's role in promulgation. From a structural perspective, does it make better sense to hold a promulgating resolution to the supermajority standards of an Article V proposing resolution, or to ordinary majority standards?)

2. *Contemporaneous ratification: The problem of transgenerational amendments.* Behind these debates are larger questions of the purposes behind Article V.

One might argue that too much time has passed for the ERA to be ratified. Congressional amendments should reflect the will of a supermajority of Americans, which must be expressed within a bounded period of time — perhaps seven years (as *Dillon* suggested), or within a single generation.

On the other hand, consider the 27th Amendment, which was the second of the original twelve proposed by Congress in 1789. The third through twelfth proposals became Amendments 1 through 10, what we now call the Bill of Rights. The Madison Amendment, as it is sometimes called, was finally ratified in 1992, and became Amendment 27. The 200 years between proposal and ratification of the 27th Amendment are many times longer than the forty-some years that have elapsed since the ERA was sent to the states in 1972.

3. *Concurrent ratification: The problem of rescissions.* A different objection is that five states have rescinded their ratifications. That means that ratification requires six more states, not just one. The argument for this view is that a valid

Amendment to the Constitution requires the *concurrent* agreement of three quarters of the states, even if all of the states ratify at different points in time. The agreement of the states is not concurrent if one of the states withdraws consent before the finish line is reached.

On the other hand, the text of Article V only mentions ratifications, not rescissions. There is also some institutional precedent for not counting rescissions. Congress refused to accept rescissions of the 14th and 19th Amendments (although it is not clear that counting the rescissions would have brought the total under three quarters of the states, see Casebook p. 350 n. 30). The Attorneys General of the states that attempted to rescind the ERA expressed doubts about whether they were effective. Aside from text and precedent, are there good structural arguments for not counting rescissions? If a state may change its mind and vote for an amendment during the ratification process, why shouldn't it be able to change its mind and vote against?

4. *Promulgation: The problem of who decides and announces ratification.* The text of Article V does not make clear who decides when and whether an amendment has properly been ratified. One theory is that as soon as three quarters of the state legislatures ratify, the Amendment is part of the Constitution. But this begs the question of what to do if there is a dispute about whether the requirements have been met. (Suppose that a state tries to rescind, or there is a dispute about whether both houses of a state legislature properly voted on the proposal.) *Coleman* seems to suggest that the issue is a political question that is left to Congress. If so, then Congress can resolve any disputes — and bestow a much needed dose of political legitimacy — by passing a joint resolution promulgating a new amendment.

The 27th Amendment offers an interesting example. After Michigan ratified the Twenty Seventh Amendment in May 1992, the United States Archivist proclaimed that a new amendment had been added to the Constitution, operating on the advice of the Department of Justice, which took the position that contemporaneous ratification and congressional approval were both unnecessary. Congress, however, passed a joint resolution two days later proclaiming that the Amendment was now (i.e., when Congress spoke) a valid part of the Constitution. Because of popular upset about a financial scandal involving the House bank, both the President and Congress were eager to pronounce the 27th Amendment ratified: this showed that they were responding to public outcry about government corruption. As a result, the case of the 27th Amendment did not provide a clear example of who would decide if there was disagreement between the political branches.

Whatever the answer to this question, congressional promulgation has an additional advantage: it bestows legitimacy on the ratification process, and may help silence concerns about whether the process was consistent with constitutional norms. The ERA presents a case in which the ratification process has been protracted, but the constitutional norm at issue has grown in authority and interpretive significance in the intervening decades. Even so, opponents might raise objections; hence, congressional promulgation might help quiet concerns about the legitimacy of the ratification process. Thus, although congressional ratification may not be necessary legally, it may be important politically. (How might this affect your views about the proper voting rules for promulgation, as discussed in note 1, supra?) Suppose that Congress passed a joint resolution promulgating the ERA, and a plaintiff brought suit under the amendment. How if at all, would or should congressional promulgation influence federal courts' judgment about whether the amendment was properly part of the Constitution?

5. *Interpretation: What would the new amendment mean?* Suppose that an additional state—or six additional states—ratifies the proposed ERA and Congress passes a joint resolution of promulgation. How should courts interpret the new amendment? Should they look to what people in the 1970s thought about what the Amendment would do, or should they look to what people *today* think about what the Amendment would do? Or are both of these irrelevant to its proper construction? Think about previous debates about originalism in this Casebook. Note that originalist arguments presuppose a bounded period of time that fixes original meaning or original understanding. But what if this assumption is lacking? Can originalism operate under these conditions?

Suppose that Congress prepares a legislative report accompanying its joint resolution offering its views about what the new amendment means. Should courts follow the views of this report? Suppose, for example, that the report says that the new amendment has nothing whatsoever to do with gay rights, or transgender rights. Should courts take this as binding or as very persuasive?

Suppose a judge concluded that (1) the long ratification history of the ERA supplied evidence of many deliberative agents operating in many times and places and espousing many different views; and (2) Congress lacked power to create a ratification history and a definitive meaning for the amendment as part of the promulgation process. How should the judge interpret the amendment?

6. *The difference an ERA makes—short term and long term effects.* What constitutional protections would an Equal Rights Amendment provide in addition to those already provided by the equality guarantees of the Fifth and Fourteenth Amendments? (Eagle Forum, through which Phyllis Schlafly led opposition to the ERA since its introduction in the 1970s, has complied a top ten list.[7])

Look at the text of the proposed ERA and consider its likely effects. Is there any reason why a judge who does not think that gay rights or transgender rights are protected by the Constitution would change his or her mind after the ratification of the ERA? What about a judge who believes that the Constitution should be interpreted in light of the contested and evolving views of the American people?

---

7. Eagle Forum, Top ten cases that prove the Equal Rights Amendment would have been a disaster, http://eagleforum.org/era/2002/top-ten.shtml (listing Rostker v. Goldberg, Harris v. McRae, Baehr v. Lewin, Ohio v Akron Ctr. For Reproductive Health, Bob Jones University v. United States, United States v. Morrison, Boy Scouts of America v. Dale, Personnel Adm'r of Massachusetts v Feeney, Parham v. Hughes, and Miller v. Albright).

Put another way, what difference will this particular piece of constitutional text make?

In what areas of law — if any — do you think adding an ERA to existing equal protection case law would be likely to make the most difference? Is the current Supreme Court likely to share this view?

Consider what laws Congress might enact under Section Two of the Amendment, which provides that "The Congress shall have the power to enforce, by appropriate legislation, the provisions of this article." Given existing interpretations of the Commerce Clause and Section Five of the Fourteenth Amendment, what new kinds of legislation might the ERA's section two enable Congress to enact? Would the state action requirement announced in the *Civil Rights Cases* apply to Section Two legislation enforcing the new amendment? Would the *Boerne* rule of congruence and proportionality?

Even if you think that the text would probably not change any current judge's mind, how might it affect political mobilization around constitutional norms? Put another way, what do you think a ratified ERA in 2018 would do — either now or in the future — in American politics, or in American constitutional law? What effect might the new text have in a generation?